MUJERISTA
THEOLOGY

A THEOLOGY FOR THE TWENTY-FIRST CENTURY

Ada María Isasi-Díaz

In the struggle,
Ada María
✝...

ORBIS BOOKS

Maryknoll, New York 10545

Third Printing, February 1999

The Catholic Foreign Mission Society of America (Maryknoll) recruits and trains people for overseas missionary service. Through Orbis Books, Maryknoll aims to foster the international dialogue that is essential to mission. The books published, however, reflect the opinions of their authors and are not meant to represent the official position of the society.

Queries regarding rights and permissions should be addressed to:
Orbis Books, P.O. Box 308, Maryknoll, NY 10545-0308

Published by Orbis Books, Maryknoll, NY 10545-0308
Manufactured in the United States of America

Library of Congress Cataloging-in-Publication Data
Isasi-Díaz, Ada María.
    Mujerista theology : a theology for the twenty-first century / Ada María Isasi-Díaz.
        p.   cm.
    Includes bibliographical references and index.
    ISBN 1-57075-081-5 (alk. paper)
    1. Feminist theology. 2. Hispanic American women – Religious life.
    3. Christianity and culture.   I. Title.
    BT83-55I82 1996
    230'.082 – dc20   96-2913
                                                                          CIP

MUJERISTA
THEOLOGY

To
All those who have taught me
what the struggle for liberation is about
All those who daily help me
to engage in the struggle for justice
YES!
LA VIDA ES LA LUCHA
— the struggle is life.

Contents

Preface

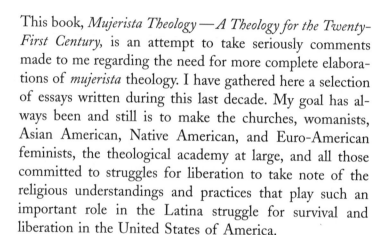

This book, *Mujerista Theology —A Theology for the Twenty-First Century*, is an attempt to take seriously comments made to me regarding the need for more complete elaborations of *mujerista* theology. I have gathered here a selection of essays written during this last decade. My goal has always been and still is to make the churches, womanists, Asian American, Native American, and Euro-American feminists, the theological academy at large, and all those committed to struggles for liberation to take note of the religious understandings and practices that play such an important role in the Latina struggle for survival and liberation in the United States of America.

And here now begins a section entitled "gratefulness," which my Latina culture and personal integrity make an absolute necessity. All of the essays but one have been previously published. I want to thank those who, considering Latinas' voices important, have invited me to write from a *mujerista* perspective an article for the books they have edited. Thank you to Letty Russell, Consuelo Covarrubias, Fernando Segovia and Mary Ann Tolbert, Susan Brooks Thistlethwaite, Ann Graff, Elisabeth Schüssler Fiorenza, Janet Walton, and Marjorie Procter-Smith.

My theological work could not have developed without the support and engagement (not always agreement) of a vast number of women. The theological work of many of them has been of great importance for my work in elaborating a *mujerista* theology. Thank you to all of them and in a special way to María Pilar Aquino, Angela Bauer, Elizabeth Bounds, Pam Brubaker, Katie G. Cannon, Teresa Chávez Sauceda, Shawn Copeland, Margaret Farley, Christine Gudorf, Anne Gilson, Ivone Gebara, Chung Hyun Kyung, Marilyn Legge, Mary John Mananzan, Joan Martin, Mercy Amba Oduyoye, Ofelia Ortega, Ana María Pineda, Jeanette Rodríguez, Yolanda Tarango, Ana María Tepedino, Tania Mara Vieira Sampaio, Emilie Townes, Carmen Villegas, and Delores Williams.

Muchas gracias to the women of the parish where I worship. Their personal support means the world to me. Their vocal prayers, shared concerns, insights into the social reality we live, their religious understandings and practices, as well as those of many other Latinas spread across the USA, are the main source of *mujerista* theology. These Latinas are indeed organic theologians, admirably capable of reflecting on and explaining their beliefs.

Thank you to my colleagues in ACHTUS, Latina and Latino theologians committed to our people, who are my main dialogue partners. Thank you to my colleagues at Drew University and particularly to the students I have worked with at Drew. Without their questions and insights my theological writings would be less clear, less precise, less daring. I especially want to thank the four women who have been my research assistants at Drew: Christine Isham Walsh, Carmen Torres, Laura Ayala, and Carol Mitchell.

The majority of the essays in this book have passed through the editorial hands of Ann Pat Ware, a wonderful, committed *compañera* in the struggle, herself a theologian, who takes care of correcting my English without making it lose its Cuban accent and flair, who always insists on greater clarity, and who pushes me to say what

I really mean when I falter because of possible negative consequences.

I also am grateful to Susan Perry, senior editor of Orbis Books, for welcoming this project and working on it with dedication in spite of a serious car accident that required her hospitalization more than once.

And the greatest thanks to my family, my kin of more than forty, who ground me and push me by expecting much of me, and who are proud of me. *Un abrazo* to all of you!

Introduction

Doing *mujerista* theology is a liberative praxis. I am an activist-theologian, and for me doing *mujerista* theology is one of the ways I participate in the struggle for the liberation of Latina women and our communities in the USA.[1] The goals of *mujerista* theology have always been these: to provide a platform for the voices of Latina grassroots women; to develop a theological method that takes seriously the religious understandings and practices of Latinas as a source for theology; to challenge theological understandings, church teachings, and religious practices that oppress Latina women, that are not life-giving, and, therefore, cannot be theologically correct. In developing a method to do theology that uses religion of grassroots Latinas as its source, *mujerista* theology puts into practice a preferential option for the oppressed. It insists that liberation is not something one person can give another but that it is a process in which the oppressed are protagonists, participants in creating a reality different from the present oppressive one. The challenge of *mujerista* theology to the churches is part of Latinas' struggle to bring about radical change without which oppression cannot be eliminated.

The goals of *mujerista* theology make it clear, it seems to me, that it is not a theology exclusively *for* Latinas but a theology *from* the perspective of Latinas that is an in-

trinsic element of Hispanic/Latino theology in the USA
and that should be taken into consideration by all liberation theologies. Moreover, for me it has been important
to work to develop a vehicle for the voices of Latinas
so that we can have access to theology, an academic discipline that influences the values and norms operative in
Latino communities and in USA society in general. I believe *mujerista* theology not only makes epistemological and
hermeneutical contributions to theology in general but also
works to uncover and undo the network of privileges that
keep Latina women absent or, at best, marginalized in the
women's movement, in Latino communities, in the academy, in churches, and in society. In other words, *mujerista*
theology is about creating *a* voice for Latinas, not the only
one but a valid one; and *mujerista* theology is also about
capturing public spaces for the voices of Latinas.[2]

The third reason for doing *mujerista* theology is to provide a theological elaboration in which Latinas can hear
themselves, can find themselves, can express their concerns,
and can, therefore, find ways to have others pay attention
to those concerns. To illustrate this I would like to quote
what a young Latina student at Drew wrote in one of her
first reflection papers.

> Something about feminist theory always made me
> uncomfortable. I did not stand for the suppression
> (oppression) of women, but I knew that I also did
> not stand for the oppression of the Latino commu-
> nity. When I learned of the womanist perspective
> through Alice Walker's writings, I associated myself
> with the concept of "a woman of color" in a strug-
> gle for her liberation, understood as her liberation and
> the liberation of her people (children and men). In
> this class I am encountering the *mujerista* perspec-

tive for the first time. This perspective offers me a viewpoint that has been created taking into consideration my understandings (those of a Puerto Rican daughter). To acknowledge this term, *mujerista*, is very important. It allows us Latinas to construct something in our own terms, not in the shadow cast by the Anglo.... I have always believed that in a struggle we must always *define* our structures and not simply accept where we are placed in the existing ones.[3]

The essays in Part I of this book are autobiographical in nature and are included here for two interrelated reasons. First, long ago I learned to distrust those who claim objectivity, which in my view is merely the subjectivity of those who have the power to impose it on others. So I have always been committed to making clear my own subjectivity as a *mujerista* theologian. Second, women's liberation theologies are enterprises done from within. Those of us who elaborate these theologies are insiders to the communities from which these theologies arise. My voice is one of the voices in *mujerista* theology; this is why the reader needs to know about me. In other words, the essays in Part I provide the reader with a self-disclosure, with a sense of my "space of subjectivity." I attempt in them to make specific for the reader the person who stands behind the words by sharing some of the formative events of my life, some of the key projects in which I have been and am involved. *Mujerista* theology is not a disembodied discourse but one that arises from situated subjects, Latina grassroots women, and, yes, even me. However, *mujerista* theology is not a discourse "reduced to such a situated subject, nor is the subject the 'foundation' of the discourse. Rather, the subject is an essential implicate of the discourse. Thus a 'hermeneutical self-implicature' that tracks the who of discourse is necessary for understanding that discourse and dramatizing its relatedness to diverse life processes."[4]

The essays in Part II are elaborations of the issues that grassroots Latinas face daily, the themes we discuss when we gather, and the concerns expressed in vocal prayers. These essays are written for three audiences: Latina grassroots women, the churches, and the academy. Each essay, therefore, attempts to have spaces — language — in which Latinas can find themselves just as the student I quoted above did. I also come to writing *mujerista* theology from a pastoral perspective: how can I say what Latinas believe so the churches will minister to us and with us, not to change us into the kind of Christians the institutional churches want, but to encourage us to put our beliefs ever more into action? Finally, for the academy to hear and understand, what I call "theoretical language" has to be used. The challenge in this is always how to start with Latinas' everyday beliefs and religious practices, how to keep them up-front and center even as I use the language of the academy. The challenge is to use such language in a way that it makes clear that "concepts 'translate' what people already know as a matter of experience."[5] So, even when I use the language of the academy, I try to do it in such a way that it does not obscure the everyday experiences of Latinas and in a way that makes it clear that in *mujerista* theology concepts, dogmas, and doctrines do not take precedence over or override the religious beliefs and practices of grassroots Latinas.

The other issue I wish to address here is that of representation. Do the essays included in Part II represent what Latinas believe? There are three issues to consider here. First, there is faithfulness to what grassroots Latinas share with me, what I observe and discuss with them, which resonates with and is similar to my own experiences as a Latina and which is what I use as the source of *mujerista* theology. Faithfulness in this regard goes hand in hand with personal and professional integrity. And the commitment to faithfulness is precisely what has led me to identify carefully the mediations involved in doing *mujerista* theology, mediations such as the way I translate Spanish into English, whose voice I choose to use in my writings, what themes I highlight and develop. It is precisely because of the commitment to faithfulness that I identify my own subjectivity and the programmatic worldview behind my theological elaborations. And to help me be faithful, accountable, I not only listen to grassroots Latinas but share with them what I write and say about them, what I conclude from what they say.[6]

Second, there is the issue of "using" grassroots Latinas. Of course there is some "using" involved in the theological process I have been describing, a "using" that I believe is part of the give-and-take of relationships. So the issue is not "using" but "abusing." Concerning this issue, consider the following. In my dealings with grassroots Latinas I am an insider/outsider. I am an insider insofar as I share religious understandings and practices, insofar as I too am marginalized and oppressed in the USA precisely because I am a Latina. I am an outsider mainly because of economic status and schooling. And, as an outsider, of course I am concerned about "using" in an oppressive way, about "abusing" grassroots Latinas. Certain things help in this regard. In our conversations I always attempt to have a reciprocal exchange of information. As an interviewer I participate in the process and do not understand myself merely as a listener, as an observer. I answer the questions; I share what I believe and how I try to live out those beliefs.

Another point to consider here is this: because I and others with whom I work are in many ways insiders to the community being researched, in *mujerista* theology we have Latinas researching Latinas. This means that the "re-searched" are, to a certain extent, in charge of the process. This is why consciousness-raising is one of the elements in my research method. The kind of consciousness-raising that I hope this work enables is the one that comes from "having the opportunity to talk about one's life, to give an account of it, to interpret it, [which] is integral to leading that life rather than being led through it."[7]

So I do know that in *mujerista* theology there is a certain "using" of grassroots Latinas, but certainly I am committed to avoid abuse at all cost. There is no self-righteousness in such a claim but rather the legitimate concern that is based on the belief that my liberation is not possible apart from the liberation of grassroots Latinas. I do what I do because I believe it is a liberative praxis, but I know that like all human reality, it is not totally pure, totally safe. As an activist, too, I know that I must risk and act even in the midst of the ambiguity that is intrinsic to all struggles for justice and liberation.[8]

The third issue to consider when dealing with the subject of representation is that of "speaking for" others. I have insisted since the very first published writings about *mujerista* theology that this theology is but one theological elaboration of Hispanic/Latina women's liberation theology. I have in no way claimed to speak for all Latinas, nor have I claimed that my elaborations are the only reflections of the beliefs of grassroots Latinas. I have always been concerned not only about speaking "for" all Latinas but even as speaking "for" any Latina.[9] But the fact is that because *mujerista* theology is about creating a public voice for Latinas and capturing a political space for that voice, there is no other way to proceed but to speak whether "as" or "for."

As someone who is an activist theologian, who does *mujerista* theology because it is a liberative praxis, I cannot assume what Linda Alcoff, a Panamanian American,[10] has called a "retreat position." As she so clearly states, to retreat from all practices of speaking for others

> assumes that one *can* retreat into one's discrete location and make claims entirely and singularly within that location that do not range over others, that one can disentangle oneself from the implicating networks between one's discursive practices and others' locations, situations, and practices. In other words, the claim that I can speak only for myself assumes the autonomous conception of the self in Classical Liberal theory — that I am unconnected to others in my authentic self or that I can achieve an autonomy from others given certain conditions. But there is no neutral place to stand free and clear in which one's words do not prescriptively affect or mediate the experience of others, nor is there a way to decisively demarcate a boundary between one's location and all others. Even a complete retreat from speech is of course not neutral, since it allows the continued dominance of current discourses and acts by omission to reinforce their dominance.[11]

The issue, then, is not whether in elaborating *mujerista* theology I speak for Latinas or not. Rather it is this: Do I speak so as to control those Latinas or to provide a platform for their voices, which are not totally separated from my own? What is the goal of *mujerista* theology, of the speaking for Latinas that happens in its elaborations? Do I bear in mind the context of what I am saying in *mujerista* theology and the location where I am saying it? Am I accountable and responsible for what I say? In other words, am I open to criticism, do I listen to it, understand it, and rectify what I say and how I say it if the liberation of Latinas so warrants? Do I keep in mind the effects of what I say, of what I write and call *mujerista* theology?

These questions are "interrogatory practices meant to help evaluate possible and actual instances of speaking for."[12] They are intrinsic elements of the method used in elaborating *mujerista* theology. They are at the heart of my programmatic worldview, of the liberative praxis that gives shape and meaning to my life.

Notes

1. Though it is culturally difficult for me to use "I" instead of "we" throughout this Introduction, I will do so as a way of taking responsibility for the material in this book. This should not in any way be seen as an individualistic exercise, for none of what I say throughout this book is something I have thought of by myself or have elaborated without the help of many others, particularly of Latina women.

2. Margaret Miles, *Carnal Knowing* (New York: Random House, Vintage Books, 1991), 169–72.

3. Teresa Ruiz, Drew University, College of Liberal Arts, 1996.

4. Mark Taylor, *Remembering Esperanza* (Maryknoll, N.Y.: Orbis Books, 1990), 3.

5. Dorothy Smith, *The Conceptual Practices of Power* (Boston: Northeastern University Press, 1990), 40.

6. In several instances grassroots Latinas have corrected me, have insisted that I was not understanding well what they had said, or that I was drawing conclusions from what they said that they did not understand or agree with. So, in those cases, of course I have changed what I have written to reflect what the women have told me.

7. Maria C. Lugones and Elizabeth V. Spelman, "Have We Got a Theory for You! Feminist Theory, Cultural Imperialism, and the Demand for 'The Woman's Voice,'" *Women's Studies International Forum* 6, no. 6 (1983): 593.

8. A wonderful article that has helped me think through all of these issues is Daphne Patai, "U.S. Academics and Third-World Women: Is Ethical Research Possible?" in Susan Ostrov Weisser and Jennifer Fleischner, eds., *Feminist Nightmares — Women at Odds* (New York: New York University Press, 1994).

9. I have up to now refused to be seen as representing Latinas, as speaking for them. I have insisted on speaking instead "as" a Latina. The elaborations that follow here are an attempt to go deeper in an analysis of my role and the responsibility that such a role bears.

10. Alcoff identifies herself thus: "I am a Panamanian-American and a person of mixed ethnicity and race: half white/Angla and half Panamanian mestiza" (Linda Alcoff, "The Problem of Speaking for Others," in Weisser and Fleischner, eds., *Feminist Nightmares — Women at Odds,* 288.

11. Ibid., 297.

12. Ibid., 301.

Part I

Locating the Self
in *Mujerista* Theology

ONE

A Hispanic Garden
in a Foreign Land

After twenty-six years of being away from my mother's garden, I returned to Cuba for a visit in January 1987. For two very special weeks, with the greatest of intentionality, I walked around *la tierra que me vió nacer* (the land that witnessed my birth), the land I have missed so very much. I tried to notice everything around me. My senses were constantly on alert, trying to imbibe every single detail, trying to sear into my heart the sights, sounds, smells of that beautiful island from which I have been gone for over half my life. The beauty of its majestic palm trees, the striking combination of green fields and white sand, the calm blue waters of the tropical sea, the immense variety of the colorful tropical plants and flowers, the exciting rhythms of its music, my Cuban sisters and brothers — no wonder Columbus said, when he landed there in 1492, "This is the most beautiful land human eyes have ever seen."

An earlier version of this chapter was published in Letty M. Russell, Kwok Pui-lan, Ada María Isasi-Díaz, and Katie Geneva Cannon, eds., *Inheriting Our Mothers' Gardens: Feminist Theology in Third World Perspective* (Louisville: Westminster Press, 1988), pp. 91–106. © 1988 Letty M. Russell. Used by permission of Westminster/John Knox Press.

Every minute of the two weeks I was in Cuba I reminded myself I was only visiting; I was going to have to leave in a very short time. There I felt the same as I feel in the United States: a foreigner. I am caught between two worlds, neither of which is fully mine, both of which are partially mine. I do not belong in Cuba as it is today under a totalitarian regime; I do not belong in the States. I am repeating the history of my mother and of her mother. Grandma came to Cuba as a young woman in search of a brother who had left their home in the small village of Tineo in northern Spain and had never even written to his family. Once in Cuba she was never to go back to her native land. My mother was forty-eight when we came to live in the United States because of the political situation in Cuba. She has never gone back and now, at the age of eighty-three, has little hope of seeing Cuba again.

As a foreigner in an alien land, I have not inherited a garden from my mother but rather a bunch of cuttings. Beautiful but rootless flowering plants — that is my inheritance. Rooting and replanting them requires extra work on the part of the gardener; it requires much believing in myself to make my life flourish away from the tropical sun of Cuba. Some of the flowers I have inherited from my mother help me to deal with this situation; others at times can hinder me.

One of my ongoing gardening tasks is to find a place to plant the flowers I have inherited from my mother. At the age of eighteen I was uprooted from my country. What I thought would be a hiatus turned into thirty-six years. I am beginning to suspect it might well become the rest of my life.[1] For many different reasons I have had no choice but to try to plant my garden in the United States. But belonging to the culture of one of the "minority groups" has meant that the plants in my garden have been seen as weeds or exotica; they are either plucked up or treated as a rarity. In general they are not accepted as part of the common garden of the dominant USA culture.

Most people think I should not find it too difficult to adapt my flowers and my gardening style — my cultural inheritance — to a new situation. After all, culture is always changing; it is dynamic. The fact is, however, that by belonging to a minority culture within another culture, the changing dynamic of my culture becomes a nonorganic force. Many of the changes taking place in the Hispanic culture in the United States do not start from within but are imposed from without. These inorganic changes do not enhance the culture but rather negate it. Forced changes bring not flourishing but wilting and dying. A culture forced to change by outside forces suffers violence; its values begin to deteriorate. A culture that is not valued, whether by being ignored or by being commercially exploited, is in danger of losing little by little its will to live.[2]

This is what happens to Hispanic culture in the United States. It is sacked and raped every time we are told that our children cannot learn Spanish in school, when our customs are ridiculed, when our cultural artifacts — typical dresses, music, etc. — are commercialized. The intergenerational crisis among Hispanics goes beyond the usual differences between youth and older people. This crisis is directly connected to the lack of importance and significance given to Hispanic culture by the dominant culture. On top of the identity crisis that all young people suffer as they search for their own worth and a way to be themselves, Hispanic youths suffer from the violence against our culture in this society. No wonder they try to hide their *abuelitas*, Anglicize their names, and join the world of drugs in order to have the money they think will bring recognition. No wonder I have never been able to plant my garden successfully in this society.

Trying to Plant My Garden

In the 1960s I tried to plant my garden in the convent. The enormous value given to family and community in my culture seemed to me to be the very core of this style of life. But, at least in the time when I was there, the restrictions on personal relationships that were part of life in the convent made true community life impossible. The emotional intensity of my Cuban culture was also out of place in the convent. The very poor and oppressed of Perú, among whom I worked for three years, taught me *too much,* and I could not maintain a lifestyle in which people talked about poverty while living a privileged life. Finally, my unwillingness to repress my spontaneity and passion led me to realize that my garden could not flourish within the convent walls.

If not in the convent, as a Roman Catholic woman, where could I make bloom the flower of my commitment to the poor and the oppressed? The search led me to the feminist movement. I was born a feminist on Thanksgiving weekend, 1975, when over one thousand Roman Catholic women met to insist on the right of women to be ordained to a renewed priestly ministry in our church. Failing, as the overwhelming majority of humans do, to remember my bodily birth, I am privileged to remember every detail of this birth to the struggle for liberation. But the process of "giving birth to myself"[3] was not an all-of-a-sudden experience; in many ways the process had started years before.

I spent the early part of my life in Cuba, where I belonged to the dominant race and the middle class. Growing up in the 1950s, I did not pay much attention to the oppressive structures of sexism operative in my country. But I was always attracted to struggling along with those "who had less than I did" — as I thought of the oppressed then. As a matter of fact, it was precisely that attraction which made me come to understand my vocation to the ministry. It was that attraction which I now understand as the seed of my commitment to the struggle for liberation.

At age eighteen I entered the convent, a protected way of life that used to carry with it much prestige and privilege. Therefore, the few times I came into contact with the broader society during the first eight years of my adulthood, I was treated with deference, respect, and even reverence. My life within the convent walls was very difficult, and at the time I did not have the lenses needed to understand ethnic prejudice. I was greatly misunderstood and suffered much because of it, but I did not have a good analysis of what was happening to me and how I was being treated by the other nuns.

By 1975, therefore, the only oppression I was aware of was the one I suffer within the church simply because I am a woman. It is no surprise, then, that it was in relation to church teaching and practice that I came to understand the dynamics of personal oppression and joined the struggle for liberation. The 1975 Women's Ordination Conference was such an intense experience that when I emerged from the hotel where we had held the three-day conference, I realized I was perceiving the world in a different way. It took a few months before I realized what the difference was that I was seeing. My eyes had been opened to the reality of sexism. My whole life had been affected; how I saw myself and what I was to do with my life had changed radically.

The struggle against sexism in the Roman Catholic

Church has been the school where I learned about feminism, as well as the main arena in which I carried out my struggle for liberation between 1975 and 1988. I rejoice in the sisterhood in whose creation I participated and am grateful for all that I learned from the women involved in the Womanchurch movement. This became my home. Soon I proceeded to plant my own garden there; however, that brought me into conflict with the sisterhood. As long as I toiled in the garden of Euro-American feminism, I was welcomed. But as I started to claim a space in the garden to plant my own flowers, the ethnic/racist prejudice prevalent in society reared its head within the Womanchurch movement.[4]

The issue was and is power.[5] Somewhat naively I had thought that together we would decide not only how to garden but what the garden was to look like, what it would be. But the Euro-American feminists, being part of the dominant culture, deal with Hispanic women — and other racial/ethnic women — differently from the way they deal with each other. They take for granted that feminism in the USA is *their* garden, and therefore they will decide what manner of work racial/ethnic women will do there.

By the time I began to experience all this, I had learned much about the dynamics of oppression and prejudice and I could understand what was going on. However, what took me totally by surprise was the inability or unwillingness of the Euro-American feminists to acknowledge their prejudice. Most feminists "believe that because they are feminists, they cannot be racists." Euro-American feminists, like all liberals, sooner or later, have come to the point at which they are willing to "acknowledge that racism exists, reluctantly of course, but nobody admits to being a racist."[6] While whitewashing — pun intended — their personal sins of racism/ethnic prejudice in the restful waters of guilt, they continue to control access to power within the movement. Euro-American feminists need to understand that as long as they refuse to recognize that oppressive power-over is an intrinsic element of their racism/ethnic prejudice, they will continue to do violence to feminism. As a liberative praxis, feminism has to do with radically changing the patriarchal understanding of power, which is operative even in the feminist movement. Euro-American feminists need to remember that, in order to undo patriarchy, we must create societies in which people can be self-defining and self-determining. To achieve that, power has to be transformed and shared.

True sharing of power leads to mutuality, and that is what we *mujeristas* ask of Euro-American feminists. It is not a matter of their allowing us to share in what they define as good. Nor is it only a matter of each one of us respecting what the other says and defending her right to say it. Mutuality asks us to give serious consideration to what the other is saying, not only to respect it but to be willing to accept it as good for all. *Mujerista* understandings must be included in what is normative for all feminists. Our priorities must be considered to be just as important as the priorities of the Euro-American feminists. All women committed to liberation must work together on deciding the priorities for the movement. This is the only thing that will allow me to continue to believe that the women's liberation movement "is one of the few parties left in town where we can all come together for the larger common cause. But if we're really going to boogie, power has to be shared."[7]

One of the easiest ways to understand the structure of power in society and within the women's liberation movement is to look at how we both construct and express

what we think. Let us, therefore, look at language. For
example, the fact that the word "women" refers only to
middle- and upper-strata white women shows who de-
cides what is normative. All the rest of us, in order
not to be totally invisible, have to add adjectives to the
word: *poor* women, *African American* women, *Hispanic*
women. *Poor* women means white, underemployed, or unemployed women. *African American* women means poor
African American women; African American women who
are not poor are called *educated* African American women.
Women *of color* in reality refers only to African American women, with the rest of us marginalized racial/ethnic
women being added on as an afterthought — if we are
given any thought at all. *Salvadoran* women, *Guatemalan*
women — at present they command the attention of our
liberal communities. After all, what we need to help change
are their countries, not the United States! *Hispanic* women
refers to poor women, usually Puerto Ricans, Dominicans,
Mexicans, and Mexican Americans. Then there are *Cuban*
women — those middle- and upper-class women down
there in Miami who vote conservative. Since heterosexu-
ality is normative in society, that meaning is also included
in the words "feminists" or "women." The "others" have to
be qualified: *lesbian* women, *bisexual women.*

As these examples show, power always rests with those
who define the norm. Language offers us a very important tool for understanding the power dynamics in society
and in the feminist movement. It clearly points out, to me
at least, where I will not be able to plant my own garden and in which gardens I will never be anything but a
hired hand at the very best. The net result of all this, I
believe, is an impoverishment of the feminist movement,
which in turn arrests its effectiveness and contribution as
a liberation movement. As long as Euro-American fem-

inists do not share power within the movement with Hispanic, African American, and other marginalized racial/ ethnic women, the movement will only be capable of bringing about a liberalization of those who control and oppress. Under these circumstances, the feminist movement might moderate patriarchy, but it will not do away with it.

My Mother's Bouquet

As I go about trying to find a place to plant my mother's flowers, I have to look critically at this inheritance. Some of her flowers are of immense beauty and value. The one my mother values the most stands for her faith in God. *Tener fe* for my mother is to be aware of the ongoing presence of God with her and with those she loves. Faith for her is a deep conviction that God is intrinsic to her life and takes care of her. Her faith in God translates into the common everyday practice of giving credit to God for the good things that happen to her and the family. That has made her come to see that, to a certain degree, what one believes is secondary to the kind of life one leads. In my life this translates into the centrality of orthopraxis instead of worrying about orthodoxy. It is indeed from my mother that I learned we must be about doing the work of God.

A second flower my mother has given me is the understanding *la vida es la lucha* — the struggle is life. For over half my life I thought my task was to struggle and then one day I would enjoy the fruits of my labor. This is the kind of resignation and expectation of being rewarded in the next life that the Roman Catholic Church has taught for centuries. Then I began to reflect on what my mother often tells the family: "All we need to ask of God is to have health and strength to struggle. As long as we have what we need to struggle in life, we need ask for nothing else." This understanding gives me much strength in my everyday life. It has allowed me to be realistic — to understand that, for the vast majority of women, life is an ongoing struggle. But above all it has made me realize that I can and should relish the struggle. The struggle is my life; my dedication to the struggle is one of the main driving forces in my life.

A third flower in my mother's bouquet is her deep commitment to the family. While growing up she knew only a very small portion of her family since both of her parents had emigrated from Spain with only a few members of their families. Out of this dearth of relatives came a great need to be close to the family she birthed. My mother often says that if all of us, her children and grandchildren and other members of her family, are not with her in heaven — well, it just will not be heaven! For her there is no way to have a good time if it does not involve a large number of us. Her involvement in our lives is continuous and intense. She expects each one of us to be just as involved as she is. For her, love has to be shown with words and action.

My mother's deep understanding of and need for family has given birth to my deep commitment to community and friendship.[8] Like her, I believe that apart from community we cannot be about the work of God — which for me is the work of justice. And the measuring rod for community is how it enables and provides sustenance for friendships. But community, like family, does not just happen. It requires intense, continuous work which must be given priority in the feminist movement, especially across racial/ethnic lines. I believe the building of a new order of relationships based in mutuality is at the core of women's liberation. And this new order of relationship must start among ourselves as feminists. That conviction is indeed based on my mother's commitment to family.

But not all of my mother's bouquet is necessarily flowers. There are also some weeds. Often, when I disagree with my mother, she gets upset, because she thinks I do not value her way of thinking and the way she has lived. But that is not true. To see things differently, and even to think that the way my mother has acted in certain situations is not the way I would act, is in no way a judgment of her. I have a different perspective and have had very different experiences. As a matter of fact, I think the difference exists in part because what she has told me and the way she has lived have pushed me a few steps farther. I believe we must take time to explain this to our older sisters in the women's liberation movement. We build on what they have wrought. If we only maintain what they have built, the women's liberation movement will retreat instead of advancing. Our older sisters in the movement must be told time and again that if we can see farther than they do it is because we stand on their giant shoulders and capitalize on what they have accomplished.

My mother has lived all her life in the private arena of the family. She has never had to work outside her home and has lived for thirty-six years in the United States without speaking English and understanding it only in a limited way. This has led her, I believe, to a lack of understanding and a distrust of those who are different from her, be it because of class, race, sexual preference, or culture. Her lack of personal dealings with people different from herself, coupled with her own personal story of having gone beyond a severely limited economic situation, has resulted in a lack of systemic analysis. For her, people are poor because they are lazy, because they do not try hard the way her mother did to give her and her sister what they needed. My mother's greatest prejudice is against those who do not have an education. She even severely criticizes people in the middle economic strata who have not studied beyond high school.

Because I grew up surrounded by this idea that people were personally responsible for the difficulties in their lives, and because of the privilege due to race, class, and social status that I enjoyed for the first twenty-seven years of my life and as a nun, I have had to struggle to make myself understand the need for systemic analysis. Three things have helped me mightily in this endeavor. The first thing was the immersion experience I had when I lived among the very poor in Perú. I often talk about those years as an "exodus" experience — an experience that radically changed my life. Those three years gave me the opportunity of being reborn; they made me understand what the gospel message of justice and preferential option for the poor was all about. The second thing that has been most helpful in understanding the need for systemic analysis and has given me some tools to do it has been the opportunity for study. Courses in economics, history, ethics, and anthropology have given me the tools to understand systemic conditions that make personal liberation impossible. Third, some wonderful sisters in the struggle have taught me what solidarity is all about by the way they have lived their lives. To join the liberative praxis of the oppressed, and to have personal relationships with them, has enabled me to understand systemic oppression and to go beyond thinking, as my mother does, that persons are oppressed because they do not try hard enough to overcome the limitations of their situations.

The second weed I see in my mother's bouquet is related to the first one and has to do with an inability or unwillingness to see sexism in the private sphere and to change radically in our own personal world the way we relate and operate. As the mother of six daughters who have had to struggle in the public sphere for all their lives, my mother understands and denounces the sexism she sees us struggling against in the workplace. Though many times she feels uncomfortable about my criticism and denunciation of the sexism in the church, she can deal even with that as long as it is not very public. But when it comes to the domestic sphere, she finds it very difficult to criticize the sexist behavior she sees there. This goes beyond the sense that we all have of protecting our own. What she finds difficult is not only criticizing her family but also seeing the oppression of women in any domestic sphere. I believe that what is at work here is internalized oppression; the domestic sphere has been her world, and she has come to see what happens to women in it as our proper role.

There is no way I can communicate adequately to my mother how much I have learned in our sometimes heated discussions about this issue. I have come to understand how much I have internalized my own oppression, not only in the private sphere but also in my role in the church — which until very recently was for me mainly an extension of the family. When internalized oppression moves from the private sphere to the public one, it becomes an element of a "siege mentality."

As a Hispanic I belong to a marginalized group in this society and have had to struggle to understand and deal with the siege mentality we suffer. The need to protect ourselves against discrimination is such an integral part of our lives that we are unable or unwilling to critique ourselves. It is difficult to see criticism as constructive when we are not valued by society. Those of us who as *mujeristas* criticize sexism in the Hispanic culture are often belittled and accused of selling out to the Euro-American women. But Euro-American feminists call into question our integrity and praxis as *mujerista* feminists when we are not willing to criticize Hispanic men and culture in public. I would like to suggest that this kind of horizontal violence is linked to both internalized oppression and the siege mentality.

The challenge that lies before me has many different facets. I must struggle to convince myself and other Hispanics that our goal has to be liberation and not participation in oppressive situations and societies. We must not give in to internalized oppression and a siege mentality. We must be willing to look at ourselves and examine our experiences in view of our liberation and continue to insist, no matter where we are, on being included in setting the norm of the feminist movement. Then I have to find renewed strength and commitment to struggle with Euro-American feminists over the issue of sharing power with all involved in the women's liberation movement. Finally, I have to challenge myself and others to understand that, as women committed to liberation, the changes we are advocating will change the world radically and that we need to begin to live out those changes so they can become a reality.[9] The only way we can move ahead is by living the reality we envision; our preferred future will flower only if we allow it to be firmly rooted in us and among us. It is up to us to change our lives radically if we want our world to change.

I plow ahead, aware that I must not idealize what I have inherited from my mother — especially because we have been transplanted and in that process have lost some of our roots and have not always correctly reinvented them. I must be careful because as transplants we often have to defend ourselves, and that can easily distort the truth. What I have received from my mother, as well as what I have gained on my own, must be subjected to the critical lens of liberation; that is the only way I can be faithful to myself and to other Hispanic women and men. The task is not easy, but the community of my family provides for me a safety net — it gives me an immense sense of security. This is one of the main reasons why, for me, hope is guaranteed and I always see possibilities. That is why I keep trying to plant my garden. That it has been uprooted several times does not keep me from trying again. Though often it is a painful struggle, I believe the struggle for women's liberation is the best of struggles, and this is why that struggle is my life. *¡La vida es la lucha!*[10]

Notes

1. In the last five years, however, I have begun to think that maybe all of my life has been a preparation to go back to Cuba.

2. My understandings of culture are greatly influenced by Geertz and Scannone. See Clifford Geertz, *The Interpretations of Culture* (New York: Basic Books, 1973), and Juan Carlos Scannone, "Teología, cultura popular y discernimiento," in *Cultura popular y filosofía de la liberación* (Buenos Aires: Fernando García Cambeiro, 1975), 241–70.

3. As I type in my apartment I face a poster that reads, "I AM A WOMAN GIVING BIRTH TO MYSELF."

4. In 1988 with the publication of my first book, *Hispanic Women: Prophetic Voice in the Church*, coauthored with Yolanda Tarango, I entered into other arenas of the struggle for justice for women, such as the academy, theological education, and the world of publishers.

5. *Building Feminist Theory: Essays from QUEST* (Harlow, Essex: Longman Group, 1981).

6. Marcia Ann Gillespie, "My Gloves Are Off, Sisters," *Ms Magazine*, April 1987, 19–20.

7. Ibid.

8. Three books that have been very important for me in the area of friendship are Margaret Farley, *Personal Commitments* (New York: Harper & Row, 1986); Isabel C. Heyward, *The Redemption of God* (Lanham, Md.:

University Press of America, 1982); and Janice Raymond, *A Passion for Friends* (Boston: Beacon Press, 1986).

9. See Sonia Johnson, *Going Out of Our Minds: The Metaphysics of Liberation* (Freedom, Calif.: Crossing Press, 1987).

10. Originally this article ended with a letter I wrote to my niece and godchild Alexandra when she was nineteen months old. In it I wished for her a life as rich in experiences as mine and the strength to struggle always for what she believes in. Alex is now nine, has a wonderful brother, Andrew Joseph, and continues to grow "in wisdom and grace," drawing lessons from her Jewish and Cuban backgrounds to help her live in the United States.

TWO

Luchar por la Justicia Es Rezar
To Struggle for Justice
Is to Pray

In October of 1967 I was invited to walk in the place of honor in a procession on the outskirts of Lima, Perú, in a very poor *barriada* where I was working at the time. The place of honor was immediately in front of the image of El Señor de los Milagros, facing it.[1] This meant I had to walk backwards! For the long hours of the procession (it went on into a second day!) I watched people praying in front of the image, offering flowers and candles to *El Señor.* Bare-footed women walked next to me in fulfillment of promises they had made. Little children were lifted on high and touched to the image. The procession stopped repeatedly at elaborate altars decorated with flowers and candles constructed in front of very poor homes. Not until much later did I realize the deep meaning this experience was to have for me.

I was at the time a member of a canonical religious community. Working in this parish was my first assignment.

An earlier version of this chapter was published in Arturo Pérez, Consuelo Covarrubias, and Edward Foley, eds., *Así Es: Stories of Hispanic Spirituality* (Collegeville, Minn.: Liturgical Press, 1994), pp. 16–20.

Full of the best of intentions, I worked very hard; I wanted to win souls for Jesus, to help people be good Catholics! I had seen my work with those in charge of the procession as a wonderful avenue to instruct them about the teachings of our church, about the Catholic faith they claimed as their own. My "missionary" mindset had been already challenged and my "missionary" zeal had been somewhat curved by the understandings of liberation theology that were beginning to flourish at that time in Lima. My "spiritual director" had advised me to spend my first year in Lima listening. "Go to meetings and listen; in church listen to women as they pray out loud in front of the statues; listen to students as they evaluate their retreats and projects." The sense of the hermeneutical and epistemological "privilege of the poor" was beginning to become a grounding principle for me.

As I walked home after the procession, I realized how privileged I was to have been part of such an outpouring of faith — the faith of the poor and the oppressed that maintains them, that is their sustenance in the most trying of situations. I felt that my well-reasoned faith, a so-called sophisticated faith illumined by the "right" kind of theology, was not any deeper or any more pleasing to God than the faith of the poor people I had seen expressed for two days. In the weeks that followed I came to realize more and more the depth of that faith. I came to understand that their lack of sophistication in explaining and expressing faith does *not* mean that a person's faith is shallow. But perhaps the most important learning from the experience was the fact that I came to trust the religious understandings and practices of the poor and the oppressed. I have ever since accepted their religiosity as part of the ongoing revelation of God in our world — in my life.

Self-Sacrifice + Prayer = Holiness?

Recently I found a letter I had written to my parents the first month I was in the novitiate. In it I described the "holiness" of one of the older novices whom I admired greatly. As I read what I had written, I remembered the deep desire I had then to be holy. Holiness in the convent was defined at that time in terms of self-sacrifice and long hours of meditation and prayer. Nineteen years old at the time, I struggled with myself to be close to God by doing what those in authority told me to do. But it was to no avail. I did not feel closer to God; I could not convince myself I was a terrible sinner; I could not see any reason for flagellating myself; I could not see any reason for thinking I had failed terribly when I fell asleep in chapel during meditation at 5:30 in the morning.[2]

The more I heard about the spiritual life, saving one's soul, the life of prayer, holiness, spirituality, the more I thought that the convent was not the place I was supposed to be. I also began to wonder what "spirituality" really meant or who besides the nuns ever used the word. For example, I did not remember my mother, one of the strongest influences in my life, ever talking about spirituality. Little by little I began to realize that the word "spirituality" was often used to set the nuns and priests apart from and above others.

In those novitiate years, the more I failed to become "spiritual" the more I became convinced that God was calling me to minister among the poor. Since all the messages I was receiving about not being "spiritual" enough did not shake this conviction, I began to question the meaning of "spirituality." Much later I came to realize that what I could not accept was the false notion that the soul is a separate entity, that one can counterpose body and spirit as if the human person could be split in two.

My uncomfortableness with the word "spirituality" and the way it is still commonly used only grew as I finished my years of training and was assigned to work in Perú. "Spirituality," for the majority of nuns and priests, continued to be equated with prayer, meditation, penance. Furthermore, those intrinsic elements of spirituality, I was advised repeatedly, were to feed my ministry. Coming to believe in the ongoing revelation of God in the struggle for survival of the poor and the oppressed only complicated matters for me. Were the poor and the oppressed not holy because they did not pray formally every day? Were those who prayed long hours, did penance, and meditated more pleasing to God than the majority of people who did not even go to Mass every Sunday?

Though I was not to articulate it until years later, it was then that I began to realize that the lived experience of the poor and the oppressed was to be the source of my theology, the grounding for what I believe about God, and the basis for understanding what God asks of me. I became aware of the fact that they were too busy struggling for food, a roof over their heads, and medicine for their children to worry about "saving their souls." Their daily undertaking to find bodily sustenance parallels the original "give us this day our daily bread," which is not a spiritual petition.

I Pray Best by Working for Justice

Since those days in Perú in the mid-1960s I have understood myself as a justice-activist. Understanding that the oppression of Hispanic women is deeply rooted in patriarchy and the racist/ethnic prejudice so prevalent in the USA has provided me with the point of entry into the struggle for liberation. What I do and who I am are greatly defined by such a struggle. And I believe that my participation in the struggle for liberation is what helps me to become fully the person God intends me to be, a self I welcome, I like, I treasure.

As the years have gone by I have accepted that for me to strive to live to the fullest by struggling against injustice is to draw nearer and nearer to the divine. Drawing closer to God and struggling for justice have become for me one and the same thing. Struggling for my liberation and the liberation of Hispanic women is a liberative praxis. This means that it is an activity both intentional and reflective; it is a communal praxis that feeds on the realization that Christ is among us when we strive to live the gospel message of justice and peace.

Following the example of grassroots Hispanic women, I do not think in terms of "spirituality." But I know myself as a person with a deep relationship with the divine, a relationship that finds expression in walking picket lines more than in kneeling, in being in solidarity with the poor and the oppressed more than in fasting and mortifying the flesh, in striving to be passionately involved with others more than in being detached, in attempting to be faithful to who I am and what I believe God wants of me more than in following prescriptions for holiness that require me to negate myself.

Notes

1. El Señor de los Milagros is the main devotion in Perú. The image is a picture of the crucifixion, with the two Marys at the foot of the cross, and the hand of God the Father [*sic*] and the dove representing the Holy Spirit above the crucifix. The devotion started a long time ago when a wall with a fresco of the crucifixion was all that was left standing in a church

after an earthquake. Millions participate every year in the main procession. Almost every parish also has its own procession. In the parish where I had been made *madrina* of the Damas del Señor de los Milagros (the Ladies Auxiliary), I was often invited to assist at the meetings of the Hermandad del Señor de los Milagros (the brotherhood in charge of the procession). Later that year I was made the *madrina* of one of the four squads of men who carry the image during the procession.

2. In an attempt to "check out reality" as I was seeing it, early on during my novitiate stay I ventured to ask some questions of Father Phillips, our extraordinary confessor who came once a month. (We went to confession every week with our ordinary confessor.) Fr. Phillips had been a missionary in China and had survived three years of cruel imprisonment at the time of the communist revolution. I will always be indebted to him for helping me to see that there was nothing wrong with me for not understanding God's will and holiness the way others did!

THREE

"By the Rivers of Babylon"

Exile as a Way of Life

It was the summer of 1961, in Santa Rosa, California, when I first read Psalm 137. I remember resonating with most of what the psalm says; I remember feeling it could appropriately voice the pain I was experiencing being away from my country against my will. After the Cuban missile crisis in 1962 I realized that my absence from Cuba was to be a long one. Shortly after there came the day when my visa status was changed from "tourist": I became a refugee. Psalm 137 became my refuge: "By the rivers of Babylon we sat and we wept when we remembered Jerusalem."[1]

I recall vividly the day I dared to mention to a friend how much I identified with Psalm 137. Jokingly she answered me, "Are you going to hang your guitar from some palm tree?" I knew that though she and many others around me intended no harm, in reality they were incapable of understanding the sorrow of being away from *la tierra que me vió nacer* (the land that witnessed my birth). At times, trying to help me I am sure, my friends would ask me to talk about Cuba. Those around me could not figure

An earlier version of this chapter was published in Fernando F. Segovia and Mary Ann Tolbert, eds., *Reading from This Place: Social Location and Biblical Interpretation in Global Perspective* (Minneapolis: Fortress Press, 1995), pp. 149–63. Reprinted by permission. Copyright © 1995 Augsburg Fortress.

out why I, who love to sing, always seemed reticent about singing "Guantanamera," the song that uses for its verses poems from the father of my country, José Martí. One of them says,

Yo quiero cuando me muera	I want when I die,
Sin patria pero sin amo	without country but without master,
Tener en mi tumba	to have on my tomb
Un ramo de flores	a bouquet of flowers
Y una bandera	and a flag.

So I kept saying to myself, "How can we sing Yahweh's song in a foreign land?"

During those early years in *el exilio*, as we Cubans continue to refer to our lives away from the island, circumstances beyond my control led me to live quite apart from my family and from the Cuban communities that were gathering in different parts of the USA and the world. And I struggled to find a way of being committed to what I was doing, at the same time always being ready to go back to Cuba as soon as it was possible. "If I forget you, O Jerusalem, may my right hand wither! May my tongue cleave to my palate if I forget you!"

Yes, I understand perfectly what the psalmist was trying to capture in the words of Psalm 137. Exile is a very complex way of life. The anguish of living away from one's country might seem to indicate how very much one remembers it. But then, an intrinsic part of the anguish is the fear that, because life does go on, one might forget one's country. "May my tongue cleave to my palate if I do not count Jerusalem the greatest of my joys!"

As years have gone by, it has become harder and harder to make others understand that though I am a USA citizen and have lived here longer than the eighteen years I lived in

Cuba, I continue to live in *el exilio*. It is today more difficult
than ever to convince my friends that if I could I would
move to Cuba immediately. It is much more challenging
now than it was in 1960 to explain to those who love me
that I would go back because I want to, and that part of the
wanting to has to do with remaining faithful to who I am.
And I often continue to turn to Psalm 137, not to try to
understand what exile meant for the Israelites and to learn
from them, but to find someone who understands me!

Meeting Scientific Exegesis

Once I had discovered Psalm 137 I needed to study it, to
find out as much as I could about the situation it was referring to, about the people whose sentiments it expressed
and who understood me. I have been fortunate to have, like
many of those who have studied the Bible in the second
half of this century, a whole array of theories and tools of
investigation at my disposal to find out about Psalm 137.
I learned how to do scientific exegesis. But no matter how
much I tried, I was not able to acquire that disinterested
objectivity that seems to be required for this discipline.
There are two things that always troubled me about this.
First, as a *mujerista*[2] theologian, a Hispanic women's liberation theologian, my hermeneutics of suspicion led me to
conclude that most of the time what is considered objectivity is the subjectivity of dominant groups who can impose
their understandings on others. Much more important than
trying to be objective, I believe, is to identify one's subjectivity, to make clear one's perspective and purpose when
dealing with any biblical text.

Second, the reason for disinterested objectivity is, supposedly, so that the scholar can come closer to the original

meaning of a text. But this seems to me to ignore that the meaning of every text is found in the interrelationship that is created between the reader, the writer, and the text. It has always been obvious to me that the richness of Psalm 137 has to do as much with what it means to me as with what it meant to the Israelites in Babylon, while at the same time what it means to me is influenced by what it meant to them. This is true not only for me but for all who study and pray the Bible. The point of entry is precisely the reader: she is the one who frames the questions being posed about the text and to the text; her hermeneutics will ultimately influence what the text is understood to have meant and to mean today. Because scientific biblical studies ignore this, they cannot get at the real meaning of the Bible. Attempts to recover the original meaning in reality turn the biblical text into an undiscovered archaeological artifact.[3]

As I struggled doing scientific exegesis of Psalm 137, I discovered two other important considerations. First, knowing everything possible about Psalm 137 is not an end in itself. The important thing regarding this psalm, and all of the Bible, is that it gives voice to an authentic faith-experience. This psalm, precisely because it is an Israelite prayer, was "not inspired by any urge for scientific accuracy."[4] Second, during my exegetical study of Psalm 137 I needed to keep always in touch with the situation for which my studies were providing insight. Scientific exegesis, I believe, should "concern itself, not with the questions it raises, but with the questions that the common people are raising."[5]

The exegetical questions I had about Psalm 137 had to do with its sociohistorical setting. I was interested in knowing the parallels between the circumstances lived by the people who originally prayed this psalm and my own circumstances. I was interested to establish a certain continuity of meaning for the text, in having a dialogue between the history of the people who first prayed Psalm 137 and my own history.[6] I knew they would have no problems understanding my love for my country; but I needed to know as thoroughly as possible if I could and would understand their relationship to their land.

I also needed to know what was behind the vengeful lines that close the psalm, a sentiment that often is also mine in regard to those who keep me from returning to my country. What was the theology regarding dealing with enemies that not only allowed the Israelites but made them pray to have the children of their enemies dashed against the stones? What kind of understanding of the divine allowed them to pray in such fashion?

Other Relevant Details of My Hermeneutics

Twenty years went by between my discovery of Psalm 137 and my exegetical study of it. Three key things happened to me during that time which have profoundly influenced my life and my perspective. First, I had the privilege of living for three years in Lima, Perú, and working there among the very poor. This was for me an "exodus," a formative and paradigmatic experience. For my biblical and theological hermeneutics, for my life perspective, the most important thing that happened to me there was that I, a middle-class white woman,[7] came in touch with *el pueblo*, the people — grassroots people who are mostly Amerindian and poor. Not only did I come in touch with *el pueblo*, but I came to value and appreciate *lo popular*. *Lo popular* has to do with what is most central to the majority of the population, with its main traits.

The term "popular" (*lo popular* in Spanish) summons images of inequality and subordination and directs attention to the poor conceived as "popular" groups or classes. References to *lo popular* also commonly evoke a sense of collective identity and a claim to group autonomy and self-governance, in particular with regard to choosing leaders, setting group agendas, and explicating the religious identity of all of this.[8]

During my three years in Lima I came to have a preferential option for the poor, though this term was not being used at that time. I did so for my own sake, for once I lived daily among people who suffered injustice and came to understand how much injustice is an all-pervading system, I realized that only grassroots people who have nothing to gain from this present system can conceive of a different one.

The second thing that happened to me was that I was "born" a *mujerista*. It was at the first Women's Ordination Conference, celebrated in Detroit during Thanksgiving weekend, 1975, that I became conscious of the injustice I was suffering simply because I am a woman. The fact that the Roman Catholic Church does not allow me to be ordained as a priest simply because I am a woman was the catalyst that started my process of conscientization as a *mujerista*. I had lived among the oppressed in Lima; now I came to recognize the oppression in my own life. I went through all the different stages that discovering one is oppressed entails: disbelief, anger, compromise, and — eventually — liberative praxis. Through it all, one suspicion was constant: what I was discovering about sexism and the process of conscientization was familiar. I knew about it, but from where? Little by little I came to understand the connections between sexism and classism (a label for the exploitative system that causes poverty). Little by little I understood that what I had started to learn about the theology of liberation and liberation movements in Latin America could help me understand about sexism and how to struggle against it.

The third event in my life pertinent to my biblical hermeneutics had to do with coming to recognize that, as a Cuban living in the USA, I am part of the Hispanic community. This in turn led me to be aware of and to understand how and why in this country I am a "minority," how and why ethnic prejudice operates in this society and in my life, and how and why the specificity of ethnic prejudice is not necessarily included in the term "racism." My process of conscientization from then on dealt with the role that racism/ethnic prejudice plays in oppression.[9]

My biblical hermeneutics, then, has as its central focus the binomial oppression-liberation. Central to it is the lived-experience of Latinas, *lo popular*. Central to it is the multilayered oppression made possible and sustained in all aspects of our lives by sexism, racism/ethnic prejudice, and classism.[10] Central to it is a liberative praxis that has our work to become agents of our own history — the challenge to be self-defining and self-actualizing women — as an intrinsic element. For this challenge to be met, we know that we have to develop and strengthen our moral agency. And that is one of the main perspectives from which we approach the Bible. For Hispanic women the interpretation, appropriation, and use of the Bible have to enable and enhance our moral agency. Finally, central to my biblical hermeneutics is the day-to-day struggle for survival of Latinas made possible by hope in our ability to bring about a different future. Yes, hope makes our struggle possible but, at the same time, our struggle makes hope possible.

A Scholarly Visit to Psalm 137

I do not intend to do an exhaustive review of the historical setting and circumstances that gave rise to the voices heard in Psalm 137. Suffice it to say four things. First, Psalm 137 "is the only unequivocal reference to the Babylonian exile in the Psalter."[11] Psalm 137, however, is not historical but rather a poetical view of Babylon. It is "a poetic picture, a general impression of nostalgia, of distress, and of a desire for vengeance."[12]

Second, the deportation of Israelites from their land was most probably partial, affecting mostly landed citizens, officials, and priests. Those who were able to stay in Judah, however, may well have been very few, given that many must have died in battle or of starvation and disease or fled. It should be kept in mind that the deportation to Babylon did not affect the population of the northern state, that Israelites continued to live in Samaria, Galilee, and Transjordan. But though northern Israelites adhered to the religious practices centered in Jerusalem, their Yahwistic religion was highly syncretic. Besides, having been under foreign rule for 150 years left these Israelites with not much nationalist zeal.[13]

The Babylonian exiles were most probably placed in settlements instead of being dispersed among the local population. Though the exiles did undergo hardship and humiliation, there is no evidence to indicate that they suffered unduly. "On the contrary, life in Babylon must have opened up for many of them opportunities that would have never been available in Palestine."[14]

Third, the biblical literature that refers to the Babylonian captivity as well as that written during that period (even though it is not about captivity) makes it possible to know how the exiled people felt about what was happening to them. Since it is hardly likely that they recorded their feelings and understandings of what was happening as it occurred, "an element of reflection and interpretation is surely present."[15]

Fourth, there is sufficient evidence in the Bible to have some understanding of the different reactions and interpretations of the Babylonian exiles as to what had happened to them. Some reacted to the disaster by turning to the worship of familiar Canaanite deities. Others turned to the religion of the conquerors, most probably concluding that the conquest of Judah indicated that the Babylonian gods had been victorious over Yahweh. A third group of the exiled people recognized what had happened to them as divine judgment and reacted with penance. This attitude helped to accept the prophetic verdict and gave them the ability to look back and produce a significant amount of biblical material, while at the same time making it possible for them to maintain hope for liberation. A fourth and final group, not much different from the third one, saw the fall of Jerusalem as a suprahistorical event embodied in the disaster of 587 B.C.E. — "The Day of Yahweh." Because the "Day of Yahweh" is to be understood as a "cultic event," its historical embodiment draws together previous and subsequent experiences of the people of Israel and provides elements for those moments — including the day of final judgment — that originally belonged to the fall of Jerusalem.[16]

What was — is — the theology behind Psalm 137? First, to understand the psalms one has to remember that Yahweh for Israel was a God who hearkened to the people in their oppression and often in spectacular ways gave them new opportunities for life. Then, one has to know that Psalm 137 is a psalm of lament in which the person who wrote it was not only expressing personal grief but was also identifying with the affliction of Israel and grieving for the community. In the literature of Israel, as well as in that of the ancient Middle East, "laments" are a literary form with certain conventions, one of them being cries for vindication and vengeance that use stylized language.[17] Third, Walter Brueggemann points out that laments should be understood as "speech of disorientation or dislocation pouring out laments and appeals for whom the orderly world has fallen apart," for those who doubt the meaning of their ordinary life.[18] Norman Gottwald adds that this disorientation is not an individual matter in a neutral social situation. He insists that in the "laments" one meets "sharp tensions, crises, and ruptures in the social order that, while coming to very sharp expression in the lives of individual psalmists, nevertheless wrack the whole community."[19]

In order to understand the closing lines of Psalm 137, the reader must also be aware of who the Edomites were: neighbors to the Israelites to the east and the south and most probably racially related to them. When Saul (eleventh century B.C.E.) defeated the Edomites, Joab, one of his generals, carried out a campaign of extermination against them. Edom remained in subjection for most of Israel's monarchical period, submitting quietly to the Babylonians in 604 B.C.E. When the Babylonians besieged and captured Jerusalem in 586, the Edomites joined their forces and were especially zealous against the Jews.[20] In 2 Kings 25:8–13 there seems to be an indication that the Edomites were more zealous in the destruction of Jerusalem than the Babylonians.[21]

Brueggemann offers an insightful explanation of what he calls "venomous passages," such as the one found at the end of Psalm 137. First, he contends, these passages need to be understood as cathartic — as bringing to consciousness and allowing expression to something that troubles one in an attempt to eliminate it. Second, it needs to be understood that when one is enraged, "words do not simply follow feelings. They lead them. It is speech which lets us discover the power, depth and intensity of the hurt." Third, vengeful speech is an attempt to make obvious unspoken feelings which, as long as they are not expressed, loom too large for one to deal with. Fourth, we need to see that there is an abyss between speech of vengeance and acts of vengeance. The former is to be valued for "where there is no valued *speech of assault* for the powerless, the risk of *deathly action* is much higher from persons in despair." Finally, the language of vengeance is offered to God; it is for God to decide and to do, not only in matters of recompense but also of vengeance, as Deuteronomy 32:35 indicates. Thus there is distance between language and action in this matter of revenge.[22]

Reading Psalm 137 Today[23]

I pray this psalm today for several reasons. First, it is cathartic, helping me to deal with the ongoing pain and longing for my country that being *una exilada* brings me. Though I am not comfortable with its vengeful language at the end, knowing how this language functions in "laments" helps me to be more understanding with myself when I find myself wishing evil on those I hold responsible for my being in exile. This includes learning to be kind to myself for, though I do not believe that at the time my family left Cuba I was capable of deciding to stay behind, I chide myself about not being all along more involved much more directly and aggressively in working to resolve the political and economic situation in Cuba. I have come also to realize that the "speech of assault" of this psalm helps me to deal with being afraid that when the opportunity comes to return to Cuba, in spite of what I have always said, I will decide not to return. But as I have come to know more and more the many groups of exiled Cubans working to change the political situation on the island — the great majority of whom constantly use this kind of "speech of assault," with a few of them actually translating the speech into action — I have come to realize that the "speech of assault" can also become the only thing people in exile do, an end in itself. Often denunciations and calls for vengeance seem to be all that many are willing to do.[24] The "speech of assault," I believe, often becomes not cathartic but rather a screen for the complicity (by omission if not by commission) of all of us in exile in what has happened in Cuba. The cries for vengeance can indeed function to absolve us falsely of all responsibility for the situation in our country.

Second, Psalm 137 also helps to sustain me even when I do not see the possibility of change at hand: it helps me rekindle and sustain hope. Though many of us have become USA citizens, the majority of Cubans in exile do not think of ourselves as Americans.[25] It is not that we are not grateful for the opportunities we have had to work hard and make a life for ourselves in this country. Not considering ourselves Americans is part of a countercultural position that serves as a seedbed for hope and spurs us on to action. It is not a matter of chauvinism but of maintaining hope.

The third reason I continue to pray Psalm 137 is for the very reason that Brueggemann says it was written:

> It is important that generation after generation... remember...that the present arrangements are not right, not acceptable, and not finally to be accepted. Psalm 137 draws its power and authority out of an-

> other vision, marked by homecoming, which seems
> remote, but is not for one instant in doubt. . . . This
> psalm is the ongoing practice of that hope against
> enormous odds. It is always, "Lest we forget."[26]

The vehemence reflected in this psalm points to our pain,
to our rejection of what makes it impossible for us to return to Cuba, to our love for Cuba — all of them passions
that keep alive in us the hope for radical change. Without
such passion, how would we be able to say to our children,
"lest we forget"?[27] Psalm 137 has helped me maintain my
identity as a Cuban so I can pass it on to our children.

Fourth, this psalm has helped me live my exilic existence
as a vocation, affirming my exile but not allowing myself
to be overcome by it, not giving in to despair and hate. If
exile is a vocation, the pain one feels must birth new possibilities. Exile must be a time for radical questioning of the
understandings and values that rooted and sustained pre-
Castro Cuba. It has helped me, after many years, to be able
to say, "There is no going back; when we return to Cuba
things cannot be the way they used to be." Exile as a vocation means that we develop a new vision of Cuba, that
we move into the future. But this future is not for those
of us in exile to decide apart from those who have lived in
the island while we were away.[28] The future does not rest
with a fractured Cuban community, exile groups against
each other, or exiles against those who stayed in Cuba.
In order to be a unified community we must forgive even
when there is no repentance, praying that our forgiveness
may bring forth repentance. But we ourselves must also re-
pent and humbly ask for forgiveness for not understanding
from afar, for judging from afar. Those exiled from Cuba
as well as those Cubans who chose exile must realize that
the liberation and justice we all seek for our country cannot

happen as long as there is hate and the desire for revenge. Justice and liberation demand forgiveness instead.[29]

Finally, Psalm 137 has taught me that injustice and oppression are also "places" of exile. It has helped me understand and deal with the situations of injustice I have encountered. For example, my "speech of assault" against sexism — against sexist people as well as sexist practices — helps me bring to the fore what oppresses me personally so that I can deal with it and, I hope, help to eliminate it.

Then, as I struggle to stand in solidarity with the poor in this country and in other parts of the world, Psalm 137 helps me sustain hope and maintain a countercultural posture while living in one of the richest countries in the world. This means, among many other things, not succumbing to consumerism, not caring so much about always having enough money that I am not generous in sharing what I have. It means that I have to influence other Christians, in whatever way I can, to understand and accept that we cannot call ourselves Christian if we do not avidly work so all can have what humans need in the struggle for fullness of life: food, shelter, health care, employment. Psalm 137 helps me to maintain a counter-cultural position by reminding me to "live simply so others can simply live."

A Modern Psalm 137

I want to finish this study by offering a contemporary ver-sion of Psalm 137. I mentioned above how the meaning of any writing lies in the interconnections between the reader, the writer, and the text, and I have tried to illumine how I as reader approach the situation and intention of the writer of this psalm and how I approach the text itself as a psalm of lament. Now I must return to the reader, to myself and what has become a new — but yet the same — Psalm 137 for me. This is no digression from Psalm 137. Indeed, I believe that this modern Cuban version of Psalm 137 completes the circle of meaning and helps us to understand the original Israelite version of the psalm.

One often hears Cubans claim that we need music as much as the air to breathe. And it is to a popular song that I wish to turn to offer a Cuban reading of Psalm 137 by those of us who are in exile. The song is "El Son de las Tres Décadas" (Song of the Three Decades), and the words, music, and original interpretation are by Marisela Verena. It was released in 1989, thirty years after the first Cubans had to leave the island.

> *Yo vengo de un país privilegiado*
> *Con la naturaleza como aliada*
> *Con monopolio de sol*
> *Antepasado español*
> *Y gente con la sangre azucarada.*

> I come from a privileged country
> That has nature as its ally
> With a monopoly of the sun
> Spanish ancestry
> And people with sugar in their blood.

> *Yo pertenezco a una raza de risa fácil*
> *Que siempre pudo reírse de cada error*
> *Subía y bajaba el telón*
> *Gobiernos de quita y pon*
> *Jugando a quien ríe último, ríe mejor.*

> I belong to a race that laughs easily
> That was always able to laugh off each mistake
> The curtain would go up and down on

Governments of now-you-see-me-now-you-don't
Playing "whoever laughs last, laughs best."

Y entonces fui la heredera de los errores
Y entonces tuve que irme de mi país
Anémica de patria
En toda soy extraña
Luchando por no perder también mi raíz.

Then I inherited all of the errors
And I had to leave my country
Anemic for my homeland
Everywhere I am a stranger
Struggling not to lose my roots.

Chorus:
Trescientos sesenta meses de nostalgia
Son tres décadas de destierro y destrucción
Treinta años de duro exilio
De extranjero domicilio
Qué pena da el son que canta
Mi errante generación!

Three hundred sixty months of nostalgia
Three decades of banishment and destruction
Thirty years of hard exile
Of foreign domicile
How sad is the song sung by
My wandering generation!

Armados más de esperanza que de metralla
Allá en Girón
Confiados en la promesa de la potencia
Los armaron y embarcaron
Y embarcados se quedaron
Quedaron acorralados por la impotencia.

Armed with hope more than with guns
Over there in Girón[30]
Trusting the promise of the Power[31]
They armed them and shipped them
And "shipped"[32] they stayed
They stayed cornered by impotence.

Salimos cientos de miles casi desnudos
Desnudos de justicia y libertad
Buscábamos refugio
Pidiendo sólo el lujo
De ganarnos el pan con dignidad.

We left by the hundreds of thousands, came out
Stripped of justice and liberty
We were seeking refuge
Asking only for the luxury
Of earning our bread with dignity.

Chorus:
Trescientos sesenta meses de andar prestados
Son tres décadas de trabajo y de tesón
Treinta años discriminados
Aunque naturalizados
Qué triste es el son que canta
Mi vagabunda generación!

Three hundred sixty months of borrowed wandering
Three decades of labor and tenacity
Thirty years being discriminated against
Even though we are naturalized[33]
How sad is the song that is sung by
My vagabond generation.

Mi tierra es hoy una jaula de gorriones
Pero un gorrión nunca se puede enjaular
Cuando vive en cautiverio

No le queda más remedio
Que escaparse de la jaula y emigrar.

Today my land is a cage full of sparrows
But a sparrow cannot be kept in a cage
When in captivity
It can do nothing else
But flee from its cage and emigrate.

No hay mal que por bien no venga
Dicen los sabios
No hay mal que dure cien años
Dice el refrán
Nuestro mal son los intrusos
Los imperialistas rusos
Y un Judas que quiso a Cuba traicionar.

There is no wrong that does not bring good
So say the wise
There is no wrong that lasts a hundred years
So goes the saying
Our evil is the intruders
The Russian imperialists
And a Judas who betrayed Cuba.

Chorus:
Trescientos sesenta meses de humillaciones
Son tres décadas de censura y represión
Treinta años de dictadura
De cárceles y amarguras
Qué pena da el son que canta
Mi sometida generación!

Three hundred sixty months of humiliations
Three decades of censoring and repression
Thirty years of dictatorship
Of prisons and sorrows

How sad is the song that is sung by
My subjugated generation!

Treinta años desde que un déspota acorralado
Vendió mi sol a una tierra de poco sol
Y mi gente con firmeza
Sobresale a la cabeza
Dondequiera que establece el caracol.

Thirty years since a cornered despot
Sold my sun to a sunless land
And my people with firmness
Stands out at the head
Wherever they settle their shell.

Chorus:
Son trescientos sesenta meses de idioma ajeno
Treinta años sin ver el sol que nacer me vió
Mi generación se aferra
A una raíz sin tierra
Qué largo es el son que canta
Mi desmembrada generación.

Three hundred sixty months of a foreign language
Thirty years without seeing the sun that witnessed
      my birth
My generation clings on
To a root without soil
How long is the song that is sung by
My dismembered generation!

Notes

1. I do not know what translation was in the prayer book where I
found Psalm 137. This and other verses of this psalm throughout this essay
are the ones I learned by heart from that prayer book a long time ago.

2. For an amplification of *mujerista* see my article *"Mujeristas:* A Name of Our Own," in Marc H. Ellis and Otto Maduro, eds., *The Future of Liberation Theology* (Maryknoll, N.Y.: Orbis Books, 1989), 410–19. Also see Ada María Isasi-Díaz and others, "Roundtable Discussion: *Mujeristas* — Who We Are and What We Are About," *Journal of Feminist Studies in Religion* 8, no. 1 (Spring 1992): 105–25.

3. See Elisabeth Schüssler Fiorenza, *Revelation: Vision of a Just World* (Minneapolis: Augsburg Press, 1991), 1–5.

4. Gustavo Gutiérrez, *The God of Life* (Maryknoll, N.Y.: Orbis Books, 1991), xvi.

5. Carlos Mesters, "The Use of the Bible in Christian Communities of the Common People," in Norman K. Gottwald, ed., *The Bible and Liberation* (Maryknoll, N.Y.: Orbis Books, 1983), 132. See also Vincent Wimbush, "Biblical Historical Study as Liberation: Toward an Afro-Christian Hermeneutic" *Journal of Religious Thought* 42, no. 2 (Fall–Winter 1985–86): 9.

6. Gutiérrez, *The God of Life,* xvi.

7. One of the most shocking things that I came to realize many years later was that in coming to the USA my race had changed from white to "Hispanic."

8. Daniel H. Levine, *Popular Voices in Latin American Catholicism* (Princeton, N.J.: Princeton University Press, 1992), 6.

9. These experiences and understandings have influenced my analysis of Cuban history, and I have come to believe that not all that has happened in the island since 1959 has necessarily been negative. Though the present devastated economic situation in the island has wiped out what I considered were accomplishments of the revolution, like advances in the delivery of medical assistance and in education, I still think that some good was accomplished. I admit that, though there has been a leveling and even deterioration of the standard of living for a certain sector of the society, there has been improvement for the poorer sectors. I, however, continue to question the cost at which all of this has been accomplished. I deplore the lack of freedom of expression and of self-determination of the people of Cuba, who have not been able to elect their leaders for over forty years. I denounce the creation of what is called "the new class," those in the higher echelons of the system who enjoy all sorts of privileges. And I condemn the preponderant influence that the now defunct USSR has played in Cuba's history since 1959. Recently I have joined those who call for dialogue with Castro, who stand against the economic blockade the USA imposed on Cuba more than thirty years ago, who denounce any violent solution to the Cuban situation. I have actively joined those who oppose any intervention by foreign powers in Cuba, affirming that it is the responsibility of Cubans to resolve the crisis our country endures, and that it is particularly the Cubans in the

islands who are the ones that have to map out the course that we are to follow.

10. Though I personally am not poor, the majority of Hispanic women with whom I stand in solidarity and who are the heart and soul of *el pueblo hispano* — the Hispanic people — and whose lived-experience together with my own is the source of my theological enterprise are poor.

11. Peter R. Ackroyd, *Exile and Restoration* (Philadelphia: Westminster Press, 1968), 225.

12. Ibid.

13. John Bright, *A History of Israel* (Philadelphia: Westminster Press, 1981), 344–45.

14. Ibid., 346.

15. Ackroyd, *Exile and Restoration,* 39.

16. Ibid., 40–49.

17. For an explanation, interpretation, and amplification of the original classification of the psalms by Mowinkle see Bernhard W. Anderson, *Out of the Depths* (New York: Joint Commission of Education and Cultivation, Board of Missions, United Methodist Church, 1970), Norman K. Gottwald, *The Hebrew Bible: A Socio-Literary Introduction* (Philadelphia: Fortress Press, 1985), and Walter Brueggemann, *Praying the Psalms* (Winona, Minn.: St. Mary's Press, 1982).

18. Brueggemann, *Praying the Psalms,* 21.

19. Gottwald, *The Hebrew Bible,* 538.

20. Emory Stevens Bucke, ed., *The Interpreter's Dictionary of the Bible* (Nashville: Abingdon Press, 1962), s.v. "Edom," by S. Cohen.

21. See also Lamentations 41:2; Obidiah 10; Ezekiel 25. Some biblical commentators see the introduction of the phrase "O daughter of Babylon" in verse 8 as a later gloss, given that the Edomites were seen as the worst offenders. It was introduced most probably at a time when the share of the Edomites in the destruction of Jerusalem had been forgotten or at least blurred. See W. Robertson Nicoll, ed., *The Expositor's Bible* (New York: A. C. Armstrong & Sons, 1908), *The Psalms* by Alexander Maclaren, 486.

22. Brueggemann, *Praying the Psalms,* 69–70.

23. I have been greatly inspired and helped in my appropriation and application of Psalm 137 by the work of Walter Brueggemann. Three of his books have been specially important to me: *The Land* (Philadelphia: Fortress Press, 1977); *Israel in Exile* (Philadelphia: Fortress Press, 1977); and *Hopeful Imagination: Prophetic Voices in Exile* (Philadelphia: Fortress Press, 1986).

24. Polls have repeatedly shown that the vast majority of Cubans will not return to Cuba at the end of the Castro regime.

25. Though the term "Cuban American" has begun to be used, it is but the tiniest minority of those of us born in Cuba or of our children

born in this country who identify with the term. The majority of our teen-age children born in this country usually say that they are Cubans born in the USA.

26. Walter Brueggemann, *The Message of the Psalms* (Minneapolis: Augsburg Publishing House, 1984), 75.

27. Moses Buttenwieser, *The Psalms* (Chicago: University of Chicago Press, 1938), 221. Buttenwieser notes that there are only three cases in the Hebrew Scripture where instead of the usual noncommittal clause "so may God do unto me and even more," the writer by the nature of the case does not shrink from uttering a real oath. This is one of those three cases; the other two are Psalm 7:4–6 and Job 31:5–40.

28. Belén Torres, "Reflexiones de una cubana de visita en Miami," *El Nuevo Heraldo* (Miami), August 1, 1992, 14A. This heartfelt article points out the differences between what the author perceives as necessary for Cuba now and in the future and what she learned regarding the positions taken and plans of the majority of Cubans in exile.

29. José Ignacio Rivero, "Relámpago," *Diario de las Américas* (Miami), July 19, 1992. In his column this well-known Cuban newspaperman refers to a radio program and congratulates one of the participants, Alberto Muller, for his stance. Muller, who was a political prisoner of Castro's regime for fifteen years, was the only one on the radio program who insisted that we cannot return to a liberated Cuba with a spirit of vengeance, but rather with a spirit of forgiveness.

30. Girón was one of the beaches in the area of the Bay of Pigs in Cuba where exiles landed and were defeated in 1962. The expedition was organized and financed by the CIA.

31. The USA.

32. This is a play on the word *embarcar,* which means "to ship" but which we also use as a slang expression meaning "not to deliver," "to stand someone up."

33. The majority of Cubans have become USA citizens thanks to a law passed in the 1960s that makes it fairly easy to do so.

Part II

Doing *Mujerista* Theology

Mujerista Theology

A Challenge to Traditional Theology

One of the reviewers of my book *En la Lucha* pointed out that I have spent the last ten years of my life working at elaborating a *mujerista* theology. When I read this, I realized the reviewer was right: the elaboration of *mujerista* theology has been and will continue to be one of my life-projects. Since I know myself to be first and foremost an activist, an activist-theologian, the reason why *mujerista* theology is so important to me is because to do *mujerista* theology is a significant and important way for me to participate in the struggle for liberation, to make a contribution to the struggle of Latinas in the USA.

What is *mujerista* theology? In the first part of this chapter, after a general description of *mujerista* theology, I will explain some of the key characteristics and elements of *mujerista* theology. In the second part I will deal with the challenges that *mujerista* theology presents to traditional theology. So, what is *mujerista* theology?

Mujerista Theology

General Description

To name oneself is one of the most powerful acts a person can do. A name is not just a word by which one is identi- fied. A name also provides the conceptual framework, the point of reference, the mental constructs that are used in thinking, understanding, and relating to a person, an idea, a movement. It is with this in mind that a group of us La- tinas[1] who live in the United States and who are keenly aware of how sexism,[2] ethnic prejudice, and economic op- pression subjugate Latinas, started to use the term *mujerista* to refer to ourselves and to use *mujerista* theology to refer to the explanations of our faith and its role in our struggle for liberation.[3]

The need for having a name of our own, for invent- ing the term *mujerista* and investing it with a particular meaning became more and more obvious over the years as Hispanic women attempted to participate in the feminist Anglo-European movement in the United States. Lati- nas have become suspicious of this movement because of its inability to deal with differences, to share power equally among all those committed to it, to make it pos- sible for Latinas to contribute to the core meanings and understandings of the movement, to pay attention to the intersection of racism/ethnic prejudice, classism, and sex- ism, and because of the seeming rejection of liberation as its goal, having replaced it with limited benefits for some women within present structures, benefits that necessitate some groups of women and men to be oppressed in order for some others to flourish. These serious flaws in the Euro-American feminist movement have led grassroots La- tinas to understand "feminism" as having to do with the rights of Euro-American middle-class women, rights many times attained at the expense of Hispanic and other minority women. As the early 1992 national survey conducted by the Ms Foundation in New York City and the Center for Policy Alternatives in Washington, D.C., called the "Women's Voices Project" showed:

> the term feminism proved unattractive...women of color saying it applied only to white women. The survey shows that, while 32 percent of all women reported they would be likely to join a woman's group devoted to job and educational opportunities, or supporting equal pay, and equal rights for women, substantially fewer reported they would join a "feminist" group devoted to these tasks. Thus we must demonstrate to women that "feminism" *means* devotion to the concerns women report, or we must find another term for women's activism.[4]

Mujerista is the word we have chosen to name devotion to Latinas' liberation.

A *mujerista* is someone who makes a preferential option for Latina women, for our struggle for liberation.[5] Because the term *mujerista* was developed by a group of us who are theologians and pastoral agents, the initial understandings of the term came from a religious perspective. At present the term is beginning to be used in other fields such as literature and history. It is also beginning to be used by community organizers working with grassroots Hispanic women. Its meaning, therefore, is being amplified without losing as its core the struggle for the liberation of Latina women.

Mujeristas struggle to liberate ourselves not as individuals but as members of a Hispanic community. We work to build bridges among Latinas/os while denouncing sectarianism and divisive tactics. *Mujeristas* understand that our task is to gather our people's hopes and expectations about justice and peace. Because Christianity, in particular the Latin American inculturation of Roman Catholicism, is an intrinsic part of Hispanic culture, *mujeristas* believe that in Latinas, though not exclusively so, God chooses once again to lay claim to the divine image and likeness made visible from the very beginning in women. *Mujeristas* are called to bring to birth new women and new men — Hispanics willing to work for the good of our people (the "common good") knowing that such work requires the denunciation of all destructive sense of self-abnegation.[6]

Turning to theology specifically, *mujerista* theology, which includes both ethics and systematic theology, is a liberative praxis: reflective action that has as its goal liberation. As a liberative praxis *mujerista* theology is a process of enablement for Latina women which insists on the development of a strong sense of moral agency and clarifies the importance and value of who we are, what we think, and what we do. Second, as a liberative praxis, *mujerista* theology seeks to impact mainline theologies, those theologies which support what is normative in church and, to a large degree, in society — what is normative having been set by non-Hispanics and to the exclusion of Latinas and Latinos, particularly Latinas.

Mujerista theology engages in this two-pronged liberative praxis, first by working to enable Latinas to understand the many oppressive structures that almost completely determine our daily lives. It enables Hispanic women to understand that the goal of our struggle should be not to participate in and to benefit from these structures but to change them radically. In theological and religious language this means that *mujerista* theology helps Latinas discover and affirm the presence of God in the midst of our communities and the revelation of God in our daily lives. Hispanic women must come to understand the reality of structural sin and find ways of combating it because it effectively hides God's ongoing revelation from us and from society at large.

Second, *mujerista* theology insists on and aids Latinas in defining our preferred future: What will a radically different society look like? What will be its values and norms? In theological and religious language this means that *mujerista* theology enables Hispanic women to understand the centrality of eschatology in the life of every Christian. Latinas' preferred future breaks into our present oppression in many different ways. Hispanic women must recognize those eschatological glimpses, rejoice in them, and struggle to make those glimpses become our whole horizon.

Third, *mujerista* theology enables Latinas to understand how much we have already bought into the prevailing systems in society — including the religious systems — and have thus internalized our own oppression. *Mujerista* theology helps Hispanic women to see that radical structural change cannot happen unless radical change takes place in each and every one of us. In theological and religious language this means that *mujerista* theology assists Latinas in the process of conversion, helping us see the reality of sin in our lives. Further, it enables us to understand that to resign ourselves to what others tell us is our lot and to accept suffering and self-effacement is not a virtue.

Main Characteristics

Following are descriptions of three main elements or key characteristics of *mujerista* theology that are closely interconnected. I develop the role of *lo cotidiano* at greater length since I have not done so before.

Locus Theologicus. The *locus theologicus*, the place from which we do *mujerista* theology, is our *mestizaje* and *mulatez*, our condition as racially and culturally mixed people; our condition of people from other cultures living within the USA; our condition of people living between different worlds, a reality applicable to the Mexican Americans living in the Southwest, but also to the Cubans living in Miami and the Puerto Ricans living in the Northeast of the USA.

Mestizaje refers to the mixture of white people and native people living in what is now Latin America and the Caribbean. *Mulatez* refers to the mixture of black people and white people. We proudly use both words to refer both to the mixture of cultures as well as the mixture of races that we Latinas and Latinos in the USA embody. Using these words is important for several reasons.[7] First of all, it proclaims a reality. Even before the new *mestizaje* and *mulatez* that is happening here in the USA, we all have come from *mestiza* and *mulata* cultures, from cultures where the white, red, and black races have been intermingled, from cultures where Spanish, Amerindian, and African cultural elements have come together and new cultures have emerged.[8] *Mestizaje* and *mulatez* are important to us because they vindicate "precisely that which the dominant culture, with its pervading racism, [and ethnic prejudice] condemns and deprecates: our racial and cultural mixture."[9] *Mestizaje* and *mulatez* also point to the fact that "if any would understand us, they must come to us, and not only to our historical and cultural ancestors."[10] *Mestizaje* and *mulatez* are what make "it possible for our cultures to survive. 'Culture' is a total way of responding to the total world and its ever changing challenges."[11] Culture has to do with a living reality, and as such it must grow, change, adapt. And our "new" *mestizaje* and *mulatez* here in the

USA are just that, our actual ongoing growing, based on our past but firmly grounded in the present and living into our future.

Finally, *mestizaje* and *mulatez* are our contribution to a new understanding of pluralism, a new way of valuing and embracing diversity and difference. Later, we will discuss the issue of differences in greater detail. Suffice it to say here that the kind of pluralism that does embrace differences is about distributing opportunities, resources, and benefits in an inclusive way. To embrace differences at the structural level goes well beyond recognizing the multiplicity of interests and identities that exist in this society and their multiple claims on the institutions of the USA. Embracing differences, real pluralism, is first and foremost about making sure that

> institutional and economic elites are subjected to effective controls by the constituencies whose welfare they affect, that neither the enjoyment of dominance nor the suffering of deprivation is the constant condition of any group, and that political and administrative officers operate as guardians of popular needs rather than as servants of wealthy interests.[12]

Theologically, how do *mestizaje* and *mulatez* function? *Mestizaje* and *mulatez* are what "socially situates" us Hispanics in the USA. This means that *mestizaje* and *mulatez* as the *theological locus* of Hispanics delineates the finite alternatives we have for thinking, conceiving, expressing our theology.[13] For example, because *mestizaje* and *mulatez* socially situate our theology, our theology cannot but understand all racism and ethnic prejudice as sin and the embracing of diversity as virtue. This means that the coming of the kin-dom[14] of God has to do with a coming together of peoples, with no one being excluded and at the expense of no one. Furthermore, *mestizaje* and *mulatez* mean that the unfolding of the kin-dom of God happens when instead of working to become part of structures of exclusion we struggle to do away with such structures. Because of the way mainline society thinks about *mestizas* and *mulatas*, we cannot but think about the divine in nonelitist, nonhierarchical ways.

Mestizaje and *mulatez* for us Latinas and Latinos is not a given. In many ways it is something we have to choose repeatedly, it is something we have to embrace in order to preserve our cultures, in order to be faithful to our people, and from a theological-religious perspective, in order to remain faithful to the struggle for peace and justice, the cornerstone of the gospel message. Because we choose *mestizaje* and *mulatez* as our theological locus, we are saying that this is the structure in which we operate, from which we reach out to explain who we are and to contribute to how theology and religion are understood in this society in which we live. *Mestizaje* and *mulatez* and the contributions they make to society's understanding of pluralism, therefore, is one of the building blocks of a *mujerista* account of justice.

Latinas' *Cotidiano* as Theological Source. From the very beginning of *mujerista* theology, we have insisted that the source of our theological enterprise is the lived-experience of Hispanic women. We have insisted on the capacity of Latinas to reflect on their everyday life and the struggle to survive against very difficult obstacles. When in *mujerista* theology we talk about liberative daily experience, about Hispanic women's experience of struggling every day, we are referring to *lo cotidiano*. *Lo cotidiano* has to do with

> particular forms of speech, the experience of class and
> gender distinctions, the impact of work and poverty

on routines and expectations, relations within families and among friends and neighbors in a community,
the experience of authority, and central expressions
of faith such as prayer, religious celebrations, and
conceptions of key religious figures.[15]

These key religious figures are not only those of Christianity, Jesus and Mary his mother, but also those more
exclusively Catholic like the saints, and those of popular
religion, such as the orishas of different African religions
and the deities of different Amerindian religions.

However, in *mujerista* theology, *lo cotidiano* is more than
a descriptive category. *Lo cotidiano* also includes the way
we Latinas consider actions, discourse, norms, established
social roles, and our own selves.[16] Recognizing that it is in-
scribed with subjectivity, that we look at and understand
what happens to us from a given perspective, *lo cotidiano*
has hermeneutical importance. This means that *lo cotidiano*
has to do with the daily lived experiences that provide the
"stuff" of our reality. *Lo cotidiano* points to "shared experiences," which I differentiate from "common experience."
"Shared experiences" is a phrase that indicates the importance differences play in *lo cotidiano*. On the other hand,
"common experience" seems to mask differences, to pretend that there is but one experience, one way of knowing
for all Hispanic women.[17] And *lo cotidiano* points precisely to the opposite of that: it points to transitoriness and
incompleteness.

Lo cotidiano is not a metaphysical category, it is not an
attempt to see Latinas' daily lived experience as fixed and
universal. Rather it is a way of referring to the "stuff" and
the processes of Hispanic women's lives.[18] *Lo cotidiano* is
not something that exists a priori, into which we fit the
daily lived experience of Hispanic women. *Lo cotidiano* of

Latinas is a matter of life and death, it is a matter of who we are, of who we become, and, therefore, it is far from being something objective, something we observe, relate to, and talk about in a disinterested way. Finding ways to earn money to feed and clothe their children and to keep a roof over their heads is part of *lo cotidiano* for Latinas. Finding ways to survive corporal abuse is part of *lo cotidiano*. Finding ways to effectively struggle against oppression is part of *lo cotidiano*.[19]

Besides its descriptive and hermeneutical task, *mujerista* theology appropriates *lo cotidiano* as the epistemological framework of our theological enterprise. Therefore, *lo cotidiano,* the daily experience of Hispanic women, not only points to their capacity to know but also highlights the features of their knowing. *Lo cotidiano* is a way of referring to Latinas' efforts to understand and express how and why their lives are the way they are, how and why they function as they do.[20] Of course there are other ways of coming to know what is real; there are many forms and types of knowledge. Our emphasis on *lo cotidiano* as an epistemological category, as a way of knowing, has to do, in part, with the need to rescue Hispanic women's daily experience from the category of the unimportant. *Lo cotidiano* has been belittled and scorned precisely because it is often related to the private sphere, to that sphere of life assigned to women precisely because it is considered unimportant. Or is it the other way around?

In *mujerista* theology, then, *lo cotidiano* has descriptive, hermeneutical, and epistemological importance. The valuing of *lo cotidiano* means that we appreciate the fact that Latinas see reality in a different way from the way it is seen by non-Latinas. And it means that we privilege Hispanic women's way of seeing reality insofar as the goal of their daily struggle is liberation. This is very important for *mujerista* theology for, though for us *lo cotidiano* carries so much weight, it is not the criterion used for judging right and wrong, good and bad. It is only insofar as *lo cotidiano* is a liberative praxis, a daily living that contributes to liberation, that *lo cotidiano* is considered good, valuable, right, salvific.[21] Were we to claim *lo cotidiano* as an ethical/ theological criterion, norm, or principle we would be romanticizing *lo cotidiano*. Yes, there is much that is good and life-giving in *lo cotidiano* but there also is much that "obstructs understanding and tenderness, allowing to appear an abundance of postures of self-defense that are full of falsehoods, of lies, that turn *lo cotidiano* into a behavior that is not open to life."[22]

The importance we give to *lo cotidiano* steers *mujerista* theology away from any essentialism that would obscure precisely what is at the core of *lo cotidiano:* difference. At the same time *lo cotidiano* moves us from the "add and stir" version of feminist theology. As an epistemological category *lo cotidiano* goes well beyond adding another perspective and points to the need to change the social order by taking into consideration the way Latinas see and understand reality. *Lo cotidiano* points to the fact that how we Hispanic women, women who struggle from the underside of history, constitute ourselves and our world is an ongoing process. It takes into consideration many different elements that we use to define ourselves as Latinas within the USA in the last years of the twentieth century.[23]

This does not mean, however, that *lo cotidiano* leads us to total relativism.[24] The fact that *lo cotidiano* is not the criterion, norm, or principle we use in *mujerista* theology does not mean that we use no criterion to judge right and wrong. As we have already said, we do recognize and hold liberation to be the criterion or principle by which we judge what is right or wrong, what is good or bad, what is salvific or condemnatory. By insisting as we have done on the "shared experiences" that constitute *lo cotidiano* we are trying to counter the isolationism inherent in individualism, the superiority inherent in claims of uniqueness, the hegemonic effect of false universalisms, all of which are intrinsic elements of absolute relativism. By saying that liberation is the criterion we use in *mujerista* theology, we are insisting on making it the core element, yes, the essential element of Hispanic women's morality and of all morality. In making liberation our central criterion *mujerista* theology attempts to contribute to an elaboration of morality that revolves around solidarity with the oppressed and the search for ways of an ever more inclusive social justice.[25]

In no way is the specificity of *lo cotidiano* to be taken as an "anything goes" moral attitude. That attitude is possible only in those who have power, in those whose social-political reality is entrenched and, therefore, do not feel threatened by the rest of humanity. That attitude is possible only in those who feel their world is completely stable, that nothing needs to change and that nothing will change. That is why *lo cotidiano* of Latinas is totally unimaginable for the dominant group; that is why they are totally disengaged from *lo cotidiano* of two-thirds of the world; that is why they are incapable of conceiving new ideas, of creating new ways of organizing society, even ways that would help them to perpetuate the status quo.[26]

Our insistence on *lo cotidiano* indeed should be seen as a denunciation of inadequate and false universalisms that ignore Latinas' daily lived experience. It also is a denunciation of the oppression Hispanic women suffer. Our insistence on *lo cotidiano* is an attempt to make our Latinas' experience count, to question the "truth" spoken by those who have the power to impose their views as normative. But our insistence on *lo cotidiano* must not be read as denying the viability and need for shared agendas and strategies. On the contrary, *mujerista* theology is anxious to participate in developing those strategies for liberation, which we know can grow only out of real solidarity, and this, in turn, depends on a real engagement of differences rather than a superficial acknowledgment of them.

In *mujerista* theology *lo cotidiano* has made it possible to appeal to the daily lived experience of Hispanic women as an authentic source without ignoring social location. On the contrary, *lo cotidiano* makes social location explicit for it is the context of the person in relation to physical space, ethnic space, social space. Furthermore, *lo cotidiano* for Latinas points both to the struggle (*la lucha*) against the present social order and to the liberating alternative which constitutes the core of our historical project: community (*la comunidad*). This means that *lo cotidiano* constitutes the arena where Hispanic women are confronted by the groups of which they are members. This makes it possible for them to judge their own personal understandings, aspirations, ambitions, projects, and goals in their lives. So *lo cotidiano* is where morality begins to play a role for Latinas.[27] *Lo cotidiano* becomes the lived-text in which and through which Hispanic women understand and decide what is right and good, what is wrong and evil.[28] As such *lo cotidiano* is not a private, individual category, but rather a social category. *Lo cotidiano* refers to the way Latinas know and what we know to be the "stuff" (*la tela*, literally, the cloth) out of which our lives as a struggling community within the USA is fabricated.[29]

Lo cotidiano for us is also a way of understanding theology, our attempt to explain how we understand the divine, what we know about the divine. I contrast this to the academic and churchly attempts to see theology as being about God instead of about what we humans know about God.

Lo cotidiano makes it possible for us to see our theological knowledge as well as all our knowledge as fragmentary, partisan, conjectural, and provisional.[30] It is fragmentary because we know that what we will know tomorrow is not the same as what we know today but will stand in relation to what we know today. What we know is what we have found through our experiences, through the experiences of our communities of struggle. What we know is always partisan, it is always influenced by our own values, prejudices, loyalties, emotions, traditions, dreams, and future projects.[31] Our knowing is conjectural because to know is not to copy or reflect reality but rather to interpret in a creative way those relations, structures, and processes that are elements of what is called reality. And, finally, *lo cotidiano* makes it clear that, for *mujerista* theology, knowledge is provisional for it indicates in and of itself how transitory our world and we ourselves are.[32]

The insistence on *lo cotidiano* brings up the issue of how *mujerista* theology deals with the past. Does *mujerista* theology pay any attention to what Scriptures tell us about God, what the doctrines and dogmas of our churches tell us about the divine, what theologians throughout the centuries have said about God? We certainly reject any and all regurgitation of the past. Reflexive use of the past is *no* good. But reflective use of the past is an important method in *mujerista* theology. Our communities have their own living religious traditions. The religious beliefs and practices of grassroots Latinas are not *ex nihilo*, but rather are rooted in traditions passed on from our ancestors and certainly rooted in Catholic and, more recently, in Protestant religious teachings.

Using *lo cotidiano* of Hispanic women as the source of *mujerista* theology is an act of subversion. Our theology challenges the absolutizing of mainline theology as normative, as exhaustively explaining the gospels or Christian beliefs. Using *lo cotidiano* as the source of our theology means that Latinas are not the object of *mujerista* theology. Hispanic women are the subjects, the agents of *mujerista* theology.

A Specific Kind of Liberation Theology. The third characteristic of *mujerista* theology is that it is a liberation theology, a specific kind with its own characteristics. As in other liberation theologies for us the unfolding of the kin-dom of God does not happen apart from history. We talk about "salvation-liberation," believing that both are interconnected and that to work for liberation for us Christians, which has to do with establishing justice in concrete ways in our world, is not necessarily different from being good Christians. For Latinas our religious practices and beliefs contribute significantly to the struggle for liberation, the struggle for survival.

Part of this understanding is the fact that for us theology is a praxis. By praxis I mean reflective, liberative action. To understand theology as praxis means that we accept the fact that we cannot separate thinking from acting. *Mujerista* theology is not reflection upon action but a liberative action in and of itself. The daily actions of our communities as they struggle to survive need intentional thinking, and religion plays a role in the thinking and the motivation for action, as well as in the kind of action done and the reason for doing it. Furthermore, the insistence that grassroots Latinas do *mujerista* theology and that so doing is a liberative praxis indicates that they too are intellectuals. The regular understanding of "intellectual" connotes a social function, a professional category. Unfortunately, however, this meaning is usually extended to mean that intellectuals, in contrast to nonintellectuals, are the ones who are capable of intellectual activity. In reality, however,

although one can speak of intellectuals, one cannot
speak of non-intellectuals, because non-intellectuals
do not exist....Each [one] participates in a particular conception of the world, has a conscious line of
moral conduct, and therefore contributes to sustain a
conception of the world or to modify it, that is, to
bring into being new modes of thought.[33]

Women in general (but in particular poor women with
little formal education, and even more so women whose
first language is not English — as is the case with many
Hispanic women) are commonly not considered quite capable of articulating what they think. Yes, many consider
that Latinas' ability to think is at best limited. It is clear
to see, then, why *mujerista* theology's claim that grassroots
Hispanic women are "organic intellectuals," that their articulation of their religious understandings is an element of
this theology is in itself a liberative praxis.

Another important element of *mujerista* theology as a
liberation theology is the part popular religion plays in it.[34]
It is precisely this aspect of the religion of Latinas that provides the greatest impetus for our struggle for liberation.
There is no way you can deal with Hispanics, study our
culture, or read our literature without encountering popular
religion. After the Spanish language, popular religion is the
most important identifying characteristic of Latinas, the
main carrier of our culture. Hispanic women's Christianity
is of a very specific variety. Its main vehicle, the signs and
symbols that it uses, and a significant part of its theology
are based on medieval Christianity, the pre-Reformation,
sixteenth-century Christianity of southern Spain. But this
sixteenth-century Spanish Christianity is mingled with the
religious beliefs and rituals of African and Amerindian
cultures as well.[35]

Now "dominant North Atlantic theology has generally regarded popular religion as a primitive force of religious expression needing to be evangelized."[36] *Mujerista* theology, as most of Hispanic/Latino theology, on the other hand, "recognizes popular religion as a credible experience of the . . . [divine]; and as a positive reservoir of values for self-determination."[37] In other words, in *mujerista* theology we insist on "the normative, graced, and even universal dimensions of the 'salvific' manifestations of non-Christian religions."[38]

Popular religion plays a significant role in our struggles for survival and liberation. Many of us know from experience that it is mainly due to popular religion that Christianity is alive and flourishing among Latinas in spite of the lack of care and attention we have experienced from the churches. In popular religion we find a sense of embracing diversity that makes it possible for very different elements to influence each other to the point where each element is reformulated, maintaining its own specificity but not without taking into consideration the specificity of the other elements.

Challenges to Traditional Theologies

In pointing out the ways in which *mujerista* theology challenges traditional theologies I do not want to suggest that there is nothing good about traditional theology. But I do want to make it very clear that its relevance to what is going on in our world today is waning mainly because of the way in which it insists on dealing with tradition, because it does not take seriously the religion of the people but seems to prefer the doctrines and dogmas of the church, and because traditional theologies seem to be content with seeing themselves as accountable only, or at least mainly, to the institutional churches.

"Epistemological Vigilance"

The first challenge is born of a need we *mujerista* theologians recognize as primary: we must have "epistemological vigilance."[39] We need to be epistemologically vigilant as indeed traditional theology should also be. But while we recognize this need and embrace it, traditional theology rejects it or simply ignores it. Now, what understandings are encompassed within this term "epistemological vigilance?"

First, we *mujerista* theologians make a very serious and ongoing effort to be aware of our subjectivity. We need to have a "critical consciousness of the limits of our capacity to know reality, and of the 'concealing and distorting' tendencies of this same capacity."[40] We work hard at being aware of our ideological biases and, though it is not easy, we work hard at revealing such biases. This means that we have to be aware of how our own social situation colors our analysis of the religion of our communities and colors the way we say what we say in our theological writings.

Second, epistemological vigilance here refers to the constant need to evaluate how our theological enterprise contributes to the liberation of our people. And here I am referring not only to the results of our theology, our writings, but also to the way in which we conduct our research. The question "Who benefits from this?" should never be far away from our minds. We need to apply a hermeneutics of suspicion to our constructive proposals, to our narratives, to our whole theological enterprise.

Third, epistemological vigilance refers to the need to avoid avoidance. *Mujerista* theologians need to be able to grapple with differences, with contradictions. We need to engage each other, to press each other for greater clarity, to question each other. In order to do this we need to work very hard at maintaining our sense of community, at not giving in to destructive competition or, what is worse, ignoring each other.

Now, all of this is a challenge to traditional theology because one of the key elements of traditional theology is its so-called objectivity, its so-called immutability, its sense of being "official" and, precisely because it is official, of being the only perspective that is correct.

Mujerista theology denounces any and all so-called objectivity. What passes as objectivity in reality merely names the subjectivity of those who have the authority and/or power to impose their point of view. So instead of objectivity what we should be claiming is responsibility for our subjectivity. All theology has to start with self-disclosure. Self-disclosure as part of theology should give all those who in one way or another come into contact with our theological work our "actional route."[41] As a theologian I am obliged to reveal my concrete story within the framework of the social forces I have lived in. I am called to reveal the pivotal forces and issues that have formed me and that serve as my main points of reference. The idea in this kind of self-disclosure is to situate the subject, in this case myself, so that my discourse is understandable to others not only out of their own experience but insofar as they have the ability to go beyond the limits of their experience and see how my experience, because it is part of the processes of living, relates to and intersects with their experience, no matter how different both experiences are. In other words, the particulars of my life might not be something others can relate to easily, but, by knowing a little about them, others will be able to find some point of contact, at least because of similarities in the processes of our lives. Thanks to those points of contact, others will be able to understand me and assess what I say without necessarily agreeing with me or limiting me to the scope of their experience.

Because subjectivity embraces the question "Who benefits from this?" *mujerista* theology challenges the so-called objectivity of traditional theology that refuses to recognize that it often tends to benefit the status quo at the expense of those who are marginal in church and society. The status quo is not a natural arrangement but rather a social construct originating with and maintained mainly by white, Euro-American males. Traditional theology offers intellectual backing for religious understandings and practices at the core of our churches, and it is easy to see who are those in charge of our churches.

Finally, *mujerista* theology's insistence on recognizing and disclosing subjectivity challenges the official status of traditional theology that results in avoidance of engagement. Traditional theology has clothed itself with the immutability that it claims is God's. Or does perhaps not that traditional theology make God immutable because it makes God in its own image and likeness?

Theology as a Communal Task

Our second challenge to traditional theology has to do with the centrality which community has in our Latino culture and in our theology. This means that we will continue to use the lived-experience of our grassroots communities as the source of our theology. So the themes of our theology are those that are suggested to us by the religious understandings and practices of our communities and not by the doctrines and dogmas of our churches. The goal of *mujerista* theology is not to come up with a *Summa*, or with three volumes entitled *Systematic Theology #1, #2,* and *#3.* The themes *mujerista* theology deals with are those that are required by Latinas' struggle for liberation. Thus, in our first book we dealt with what grounds the struggle for many of us, our understanding of God.[42] The second book dealt with issues of self-identity — of ethnicity — and of moral agency.[43] And now we are working on issues of embodiment, for what is most commonly used against us, to oppress us, is our bodies.[44]

Yes, we need to continue to approach theology from the perspective of the religious understandings and practices of our communities. This means that we must resist the temptation to do theology as usual, not only by using different methods but also by resisting the temptation to follow the "regular" themes and divisions of traditional theology. In no way does this mean that our theology is not, should not be rigorous. We owe to ourselves and our communities the very best theology that we can do. But good theology for us *mujerista* theologians is a theology that helps our people in their struggle for survival, not a theology that receives the blessing of the status quo because it follows traditional patterns.

In a way traditional theology, even the best of traditional theology, by insisting on following the patterns established long ago in my opinion, closes itself to the ongoing revelation of the divine in our midst. Those who do traditional theology call their way of proceeding "faithfulness to the past." I call it "blindness to the present" and "ignoring the God-in-our-midst today."

The Importance of Differences

A third challenge *mujerista* theology presents to traditional theology has to do with *mestizaje* and *mulatez,* with how we understand and deal with diversity, with differences. For us differences are not something to be done away with but rather something to be embraced. In our theology we do not aim at assimilation, at making all that is different fit into some preconceived norm or center. That is not how we deal with diversity. Both our understanding of *mestizaje* and *mulatez* as well as our understanding of popular religion and how it functions in *mujerista* theology make explicit what we mean when we talk about embracing diversity.

Let me explain this further here. Usually in mainline discourse, in traditional theological discourse, difference is defined as absolute otherness, mutual exclusion, categorical opposition.[45] This is an essentialist meaning of difference in which one group serves as the norm against which all others are to be measured. Those of us who do not measure up are considered to be deviant, and our ideas are heretical. Difference of opinion, difference of perspective, arising most of the time from different life-experiences, any and all differences are defined as exclusion and opposition.

This way of defining difference expresses a fear of specificity and a fear of making permeable the boundaries between oneself and the others, between one's ideas and those of others. Specificity tends to be understood as unique — lending it a certain air of "the unknown" of which one is afraid or which is romanticized as exotic.

In *mujerista* theology we posit embracing differences as a moral option. We work at seeing those who are different from us as mirrors of ourselves and what we think. Ideas that are different from ours are mirrors — not the only ones — we have for our ideas (ideas similar to ours, of course, also are mirrors of our ideas) for they do make us see our ideas in a new light, maybe even make it possible for us to better understand our own ideas, to clarify them for ourselves and for others, a result that might not be achieved if we were to ignore ideas different from ours.

To embrace differences we have to stop being lazy and have to know what others really think. But that requires self-conscious interaction, and we are afraid of interacting with those with whom we disagree. Also, to be able to interact with others we have to affirm difference as something positive, we have to affirm plurality, to make permeable the boundaries of our categories. All of this requires embracing ambiguity, something those of us who live at the margins know much about. But traditional theology is not willing to do that because instead of risking ambiguity it rests secure in its impermeable and immutable center.

In *mujerista* theology difference, then, means not otherness or exclusive opposition but specificity and heterogeneity. Difference is understood as relational rather than as a matter of substantive categories and attributes. Difference is not then a description of categories, descriptions set one against the other across a barbed wire fence. Rather difference points to the specificity of each description and seeks ways to relate those different descriptions, different because they come from people with dissimilar life-experiences.

Embracing difference, welcoming ambiguity, is not in any way to be conceived as wishy-washiness! We are not advocating total relativity. As a matter of fact because *mujerista* theology is a strategy for liberation, there is a certain discipline of action that we demand of each other. Also, in Latino culture tradition is something very important. So tradition is taken into consideration. But the role of tradition is not to impose itself perennially without any changes. The role of tradition is to make present the wisdom of generations past which we are then called to evaluate and apply to the present in view of our need for survival, our need for liberation. And, unfortunately, that is an understanding of tradition that traditional theology is not willing to consider.

Conclusion

In many ways what has guided *mujerista* theology from the beginning are those wonderful words of Miriam in the book of Numbers, "Has Yahweh indeed spoken only through Moses?" (Num. 12:2). Well aware of the fact that she suffered severe penalties for daring to scold Moses, for daring to claim that Yahweh also spoke to her and through her, our sister Miriam invites *mujerista* theologians to throw our lot with the people of God and to hope that, just as in her case, the authorities will catch up with us, that they will eventually also see that we have no leprosy, that we are clean. But their declaration of cleanliness is *not* what makes us clean; their saying is *not* what makes *mujerista* theology a worthwhile and important task for us. It is rather the fact that *mujerista* theology is part of the struggle for survival, the struggle for liberation — that is what makes it right and just for us to pursue it. Doing *mujerista* theology is an intrinsic element of our struggle, of our lives, because indeed, for Latinas in the USA to struggle is to live, *la vida es la lucha*.

Notes

1. There is no agreement among Latinas whether to refer to ourselves as "Hispanic women" or as "Latina women." My choosing to use "Latina" is done indiscriminately.

2. In *mujerista* theology heterosexism is understood to be a distinct element of sexism.

3. It is important to notice that we do *not* use the term *mujerismo* since it can be understood to indicate that Latinas' natural entity is based on being woman when in fact our natural entity as women is based on being human. See Raquel Rodríguez, "La marcha de las mujeres...," *Pasos,* no. 344 (March–April 1991): 11, n. 6.

4. Linda Williams, "Ending the Silences: The Voices of Women of Color," *Equal Means* 1, no. 4 (Winter 1993): 13.

5. Though the rest of this chapter refers more directly to *mujerista* Latinas, we intend here to make explicit that Latino men as well as men and women from other racial/ethnic groups can also opt to be *mujeristas.*

6. Rosa Marta Zárate Macías, "Canto de mujer," in *Concierto a mi pueblo,* tape produced by Rosa Marta Zárate Macías, P.O. Box 7366, San Bernardino, CA 92411. Much of this description is based on this song composed and interpreted by Rosa Marta in response to several Latinas' insistence on the need for a song that would help to express who they are and that would inspire them in the struggle. For the full text of her song in English and Spanish see Ada María Isasi-Díaz, "*Mujeristas:* A Name of Our Own," *Christian Century* (May 24–31, 1989): 560–62.

7. Our usage of these words goes beyond their original meaning to include the mixing of Hispanics/Latinos in the USA with those of other races-cultures who live in this country, and the mixing among ourselves, Hispanics/Latinos coming from different countries of Latin America and the Caribbean.

8. I use *mulato* and *mulata* in Spanish to indicate that the social connotation that we give to this word is not as derogatory as the one given to it in the USA. By using the Spanish spelling I also seek not to offend African Americans in this country who find the use of the word "mulatto" offensive.

9. Justo L. González, "Hispanics in the United States," *Listening — Journal of Religion and Culture* 27, no. 1 (Winter 1992): 14.

10. Ibid., 15.

11. Ibid.

12. Michael Parenti, *Power and the Powerless* (New York: St. Martin's Press, 1978), 28.

13. Otto Maduro, *Religion and Social Conflict* (Maryknoll, N.Y.: Orbis Books, 1982), 42–43.

14. I use "kin-dom" to avoid using the sexist and elitist word "kingdom." Also, the sense of family of God that "kin-dom" represents is much in line with the centrality of family in our Latina culture. I am grateful to Georgene Wilson, O.S.F., from whom I learned this word.

15. Daniel H. Levine, *Popular Voices in Latin American Catholicism* (Princeton, N.J.: Princeton University Press, 1992), 317.

16. Ibid.

17. This has very serious methodological implications for *mujerista* theology. See Ada María Isasi-Díaz, *En la Lucha — Elaborating a Mujerista Theology* (Minneapolis: Fortress Press, 1993), chapter 3.

18. Sharon Welch, "Sporting Power — American Feminists, French Feminists and an Ethic of Conflict," in C. W. Maggie Kim, Susan M. St. Ville, and Susan M. Simonaitis, eds., *Transfigurations: Theology and the French Feminists* (Minneapolis: Fortress Press, 1993), 174.

19. I want to make absolutely clear that *lo cotidiano* is not to be understood as housekeeping chores in the sense that women's daily work is usually conceptualized: cleaning, doing laundry, driving the children to extracurricular activities. However, neither do I wish to diminish the importance of those kinds of tasks.

20. Otto Maduro, *Mapas para la fiesta* (Buenos Aires: Centro Nueva Tierra para la Promoción Social y Pastoral, 1992), 17.

21. In *mujerista* theology salvation and liberation are intrinsically united. There can be no salvation without liberation. The realization of the kin-dom of God, which is what salvation refers to, begins to be a reality in history, and that is what liberation is. Liberation has to do with full-ness of life, a prerequisite of the full realization of the kin-dom of God. For a fuller explanation see *En la Lucha*, 34–45.

22. Ivone Gebara, *Conhece-te a ti misma* (São Paulo: Ediciones Paulinas, 1991), 24.

23. For an explanation of the elements that are key to the self-understanding of Latinas see *En la Lucha*.

24. My main dialogue partners for these following paragraphs have been Margaret Farley and Leonardo Boff, whom I cite below. See Margaret Farley, "Feminism and Universal Morality," in Gene Outka and John P. Reeder, eds., *Prospect for a Common Morality* (Princeton, N.J.: Princeton University Press, 1993): 170–90.

25. Leonardo Boff, "La postmodernidad y la miseria de la razón liberadora," *Pasos* 54 (July–August 1994): 13.

26. Ibid., 13. I am reminded here of one of the reasons Míguez Bonino gives for the preferential option for the poor and oppressed. According to him since they have nothing to gain from the present structures, the poor and the oppressed are capable of imagining a different future, something those who are set in protecting the present are not capable of doing. See José Míguez Bonino, "Nuevas tendencias en teología," *Pasos* 9 (January 1987): 22.

27. Cecilia Mino G., "Algunas reflexiones sobre pedagogía de género y cotidianidad," *Tejiendo Nuestra Red* 1, no. 1 (October 1988): 11–12.

28. To claim *lo cotidiano* as lived-text is in no way to say that it is a moral criterion.

29. Though I do not agree with all of Mary McClintock Fulkerson's ideas, her book gives much to think about in our own *mujerista* theological enterprise. See her book *Changing the Subject: Women's Discourses and Feminist Theology* (Minneapolis: Fortress Press, 1994).

30. Maduro, *Mapas para la fiesta*, 137.

31. And in *mujerista* theology we are very clear about our partisan perspective. We make a clear option for the perspective of Latinas based on the fact that we believe the Christian message of justice and peace is based on an option for the oppressed.

32. I have here adapted Maduro's synthesis about knowledge. See *Mapas para la fiesta*, 136–38.

33. Antonio Gramsci, *Prison Notebook,* ed. and trans. Quintin Hoare and Geoffrey Norwell Smith (New York: International Publishers, 1975), 9.

34. Generally popular religion is understood along the lines of less sophisticated, nonsystematic, almost dealing with magic. Here it means nothing of that but simply refers to "the religion of the people."

35. At present certain Pentecostal elements are beginning to be integrated into Latino popular religion.

36. Arturo Bañuelas, "U.S. Hispanic Theology," *Missiology* 20, no. 2 (April 1992): 290–91.

37. Ibid.

38. This quotation is taken from unpublished notes of Orlando Espín and Sixto García for a presentation they made at the Catholic Theological Society of America. An edited version of their presentation/workshop can be found in the *Catholic Theological Society of America Proceedings* 42 (1987): 114–19.

39. This term is used by Maduro. In his work it refers mainly to the meaning I notice in the next paragraph. See Maduro, *Religion and Social Conflict,* 27–29.

40. Ibid., 27.

41. Mark Kline Taylor, *Remembering Esperanza* (Maryknoll, N.Y.: Orbis Books, 1990), 1–18.

42. Ada María Isasi-Díaz and Yolanda Tarango, *Hispanic Women: Prophetic Voice in the Church* (San Francisco: Harper & Row, 1988; reprint, Minneapolis: Fortress Press, 1992).

43. *En la Lucha.*

44. We are in the process of doing reflection weekends with Latinas all around the country to collect material on how Latinas understand and relate to our bodies.

45. I am indebted to the work of Iris Marion Young on the issue of diversity. See Iris Marion Young, *Justice and the Politics of Difference* (Princeton, N.J.: Princeton University Press, 1990), particularly chapter 6.

Solidarity

Love of Neighbor in the Twenty-First Century

My next door neighbor when I lived as a missionary in Perú was a family with four precious children.[1] They lived in a hut-like house with no plumbing and no electricity. The father, Cáceres, who worked as a painter when there was work, was an outgoing person who always had time to talk to me as I passed by his house on my way to catch the bus.[2] One day he asked me why I had left Cuba and the United States to become a missionary. I tried to explain to him the sense of vocation that impelled me to live among the poor and to struggle for justice. At the end of our conversation as I was walking away, Cáceres called out to me and said, "Remember, you can always leave this place; we can't." Cáceres's words have stayed with me and have helped me understand several things: my work is not a doing for others but, as far as possible, a being with others. The goal is not to be like the poor and the oppressed (an impossibility), but rather to be in solidarity with them. Cáceres's words were one of the initial reasons

An earlier version of this chapter was published as "Solidarity: Love of Neighbor in the 1980s" in Susan Brooks Thistlethwaite and Mary Potter Engel, eds., *Lift Every Voice: Constructing Christian Theologies from the Underside* (San Francisco: HarperCollins, 1990), pp. 31–40.

why I have been concerned with understanding what solidarity is about and how to live in solidarity with the poor and the oppressed.

Many years after my conversation with Cáceres I was at one of the largest church-oriented women's conferences in the United States. A number of the participants had asked the organizers for an opportunity to address the gathering about a variety of justice issues in which they were involved. At the last plenary session all those who wanted to speak were lined up and allowed to speak for no more than three minutes each. I was struck particularly by a woman who advocated opposition to the Contras in Nicaragua.[3] She asked us "to be in solidarity with the Sandinista government." She herself was totally committed to the Sandinista cause and worked very hard in favor of the people of Nicaragua. She was indeed in solidarity with the struggles of the Nicaraguans against the Contras. What struck me was the response to her plea: applause. As I looked around I suspected that many of the people who had applauded were being very sincere, that they really agreed with what she was saying. But I also suspected and continue to suspect that for the majority of people who are committed to justice, solidarity means agreement with and sympathy for the poor and the oppressed.

After this experience at the women's conference I began to be concerned about how the word "solidarity" is used and misused. I am convinced that its meaning has been coopted. What worries me most is that "solidarity" is understood as a disposition: one can have it for a while, put it aside for whatever reason, and then pick it up again. I am also worried about the fact that "solidarity" has come to mean "agreement with" and that it is given an ephemeral sense of supporting others that has little or nothing to do with liberative praxis.[4]

It is my contention that solidarity, in the original sense of that word, must replace charity as the appropriate Christian behavior — ethical behavior — in our world today. This contention implies a significant paradigmatic shift for Christian behavior, for there is an essential difference between solidarity and charity. Charity, the word used most often when talking about love of neighbor, has been implemented mainly through a one-sided giving, a donation almost always, of what we have in abundance. Obviously that is not all that charity means, but, in general, this is how it is understood and used. I am not saying that giving is not an appropriate, even a necessary way of loving. I do believe, however, that giving is an ethical behavior today only if it is understood and carried out within the context of solidarity.

The paradigmatic shift I am proposing calls for solidarity as the appropriate present-day expression of the gospel mandate that we love our neighbor. This commandment, which encapsulates the gospel message, is the goal of Christianity.[5] I believe salvation depends on love of neighbor, and because love of neighbor today should be expressed through solidarity, solidarity can and should be considered the *sine qua non* of salvation. This means that we have to be very clear about who "our neighbor" is. Our neighbor, according to Matthew 25, is the least of our sisters and brothers. Neighbors are the poor, the oppressed, for whom we must have a preferential option. This we cannot have apart from being in solidarity with them.[6]

The Original (True) Meaning of Solidarity

The true meaning of solidarity has been under serious attack; it has been diluted. As proof, notice how fashionable

the usage of "solidarity" has become, how easily it rolls
off the tongues of all sorts of speakers, how unthreaten-
ing it is. If the true meaning of solidarity were understood
and intended, visible radical change would be happening
in the lives of all of us who endorse it with our applause.
Solidarity is not a matter of agreeing with, of supporting,
liking, or being inspired by the cause of a group of people.
Though all these might be part of solidarity, solidarity goes
beyond all of them. Solidarity has to do with understanding the interconnections that exist between oppression and
privilege, between the rich and the poor, the oppressed and
the oppressors. It also refers to the cohesiveness that needs
to exist among communities of struggle.

Solidarity is the union of kindred persons "arising
from the common responsibilities and interests, as between classes, peoples, or groups; community of interests,
feelings, purposes, or action; social cohesion."[7] Solidarity
moves away from the false notion of disinterest, of doing
for others in an altruistic fashion. Instead it is grounded in
"common responsibilities and interests," which necessarily
arouse shared feelings and lead to joint action.

From a Christian perspective the goal of solidarity is
to participate in the ongoing process of liberation through
which we Christians become a significantly positive force
in the unfolding of the "kin-dom" of God.[8] At the center of the unfolding of the kin-dom is the salvific act of
God. Salvation and liberation are interconnected. Salvation
is gratuitously given by God; it flows from the very essence
of God: love. Salvation is worked out through the love
between God and each human being and among human
beings. This love relationship is the goal of all life — it
constitutes the fullness of humanity.[9] Therefore, love sets
in motion and sustains the ongoing act of God's salvation in which each person necessarily participates, since

love requires, per se, active involvement of those who are in relationship.

Our participation in the act of salvation is what we refer to as liberation. It consists of our work to transform the world. Liberation is both cause and effect of the struggle to have a love relationship with others, including God. Now, there can be no salvation without liberation, though no single act of liberation can be totally identified with salvation in its fullness. As Gustavo Gutiérrez has said, "Without liberating historical events, there would be no growth of the Kingdom [*sic*]...we can say that the historical, political, liberating event is the growth of the Kingdom [*sic*] and is a salvific event; but it is not the coming of the Kingdom [*sic*], not all of salvation."[10]

The main obstacle to the unfolding of the kin-dom is the alienation from God and from each other experienced by all in and through the oppressive societal categories and structures that cause and sustain oppression.[11] This alienation is what we refer to as sin, both personal sin and structural sin. Sin affects the totality of the person and the relationship with God and with others. Sin always affects society; it is a concrete historical reality brought about and sustained by personal behavior that is institutionalized and sanctioned by societal norms. "Sin appears, therefore, as the fundamental alienation, the root of a situation of injustice and exploitation."[12]

To struggle against oppression, against alienation, is a matter of an ongoing personal conversion that involves effective attempts to change alienating societal structures. This personal conversion cannot happen apart from solidarity with the oppressed. But why are the poor and the oppressed those with whom we must be in solidarity? Why does overcoming alienation demand a preferential option for the oppressed? The reason is not that the poor and the oppressed are morally superior. Those who are oppressed are not personally better or more innocent or purer in their motivations than the rest of us. The preferential option at the heart of solidarity is based on the fact that the point of view of the oppressed, "pierced by suffering and attracted by hope, allows them, in their struggles, to conceive another reality. Because the poor suffer the weight of alienation, they can conceive a different project of hope and provide dynamism to a new way of organizing human life for all."[13] This contribution, which they alone can give, makes it possible for everyone to overcome alienation. The preferential option for the poor and the oppressed makes it possible for the oppressors to overcome alienation, because to be oppressive limits love, and love cannot exist in the midst of alienation. Oppression and poverty must be overcome because they are "a slap in the face of God's sovereignty."[14] The alienation they cause is a denial of God. Gutiérrez refers to the profoundly biblical insight of a Bolivian campesino: "an atheist is someone who fails to practice justice toward the poor."[15]

Who are the poor and oppressed for whom we must opt, with whom we must be in solidarity? They are the ones who are exploited, who suffer systemic violence, the victims of cultural imperialism. The poor and the oppressed are those for whom the struggle for survival is a way of life. To be poor and oppressed means "to die of hunger, to be illiterate, to be exploited by others, not to know that you are being exploited, not to know you are a person."[16] The poor and the oppressed are marginalized, powerless. They are those who suffer from specific forms of oppression — sexism, racism/ethnic prejudice, classism. These specific oppressions, however, are not self-contained realities but are interconnected parts of a worldwide system of domination in which the few oppress the many.[17] This system of domination permeates every aspect of society: ideology, religion, social mores, government, businesses, families, relationships.

Solidarity as Theory and Strategy for Liberation

As an effective way of opposing systems of oppression, we must understand solidarity both as a theory and as a strategy.[18] As a theory solidarity opposes the theory of oppression[19] by reconceptualizing every aspect of society. Control and domination, which I believe are the main characteristics of oppressive structures and relationships, cease to be key elements of societal structures; they cease to be the way people relate to each other. Instead, a new order of relationship makes it possible for a commonality of feelings and interests to flourish and becomes the cornerstone of society, the way it is organized and operates. As a strategy, then, solidarity brings about radical societal change. In our world today, hardly any society is isolated. Therefore, to bring about radical change in one society requires insights and strategies that can effectively undo and replace control and domination with communality of feelings and interests worldwide.

The starting place of solidarity as a theory is not a generalized conception of oppression that easily becomes an abstraction. The starting place of the theory of solidarity has to be the oppression of specific persons, oppression caused or maintained, directly or indirectly, by the privileges of the oppressors. Only because the theory of solidarity is grounded in particular forms of oppression can we claim that solidarity involves understanding and undoing the connections between different forms of oppression. These connections among forms of oppression indicate that there must be commonality of interests among the oppressed, which in turn points to the possibility and need for mutuality among them. If there is no mutuality among the oppressed, they can very easily become tomorrow's oppressors. Without real mutuality we run the risk of not bringing about structural change but rather of promoting participation of the oppressed in present structures.

The theoretical aspect of solidarity is intrinsically linked to solidarity as a strategy.[20] In other words, solidarity on the one hand is a strategy that consists of a praxis of mutuality. On the other hand, solidarity is an understanding and worldview, a theory, about the commonality of interests that links humanity. The praxis of mutuality, the strategic aspect of solidarity, implements the theory of solidarity at the same time that it provides the ground for the reflection needed to elaborate further the theory of solidarity. The theoretical aspect of solidarity provides a goal for the strategy of solidarity: recognition of commonality of interests. This goal, in turn, becomes an inherent way for evaluating how mutuality is functioning as a strategy. Solidarity as a strategy demands an ever greater clarity about the meaning of "commonality of interests." As a strategy solidarity requires such understanding to be specific and historically rooted. "Commonality of interests" cannot be an abstraction; its specificity is defined by the social, economic, and political circumstances of the persons affected by such commonality or its absence. The inseparable internal relation of theory to strategy that I am claiming for solidarity necessitates a dialogic, circular understanding of the elements of solidarity: commonality of interests and mutuality. Neither of these elements is to be considered more important or more necessary than the other. They are inexorably bound; each of them is always understood in view of the other. There is no separation or opposition,

no dichotomy or dialectical relationship between mutuality
and commonality of interest.

Mutuality as the Strategy for Solidarity

Common interests — that view of the fate of our world
that grounds solidarity — are what move Christian behavior
from the one-sidedness of charity to mutuality. Common
interests and mutuality can make effective in our lives the
"love your neighbor as yourself" that is central to the gospel
message of love and justice. In our world today the interconnections that exist among nations and peoples in
different parts of the planet make obvious the need for embracing commonality of interests as an important goal. Two
world wars, multinational corporations, the threat of global
annihilation, the global spread of AIDS, the worldwide political influence and control of the superpowers, acid rain,
the deterioration of the ozone layer — all these point to the
interconnections operating in our world today. The task of
those of us interested in making solidarity a reality is to
bring about a mutuality among peoples that will make clear
such common interests.

First let us look at how to bring about a praxis of mutuality among the oppressed. Mutuality has to be preceded
by conscientization. This is a process during which one
becomes aware, starting with no more than a moment of
insight, that there is something suspicious about one's oppressed condition. Almost anything can create the spark
that moves people "from a 'naive awareness,' which does
not deal with problems, gives too much value to the past,
tends to accept mythical explanations, and tends toward
debate, to a 'critical awareness,' which delves into problems,
is open to new ideas, replaces magical explanations with

real causes, and tends to dialogue."[21] Paulo Freire insists that this process of conscientization involves praxis and is not just an intellectual understanding apart from action.[22] Conscientization makes the oppressed understand the real causes of oppression and the need to engage with others in changing such a situation. This process of conscientization is not something that happens once and for all. Conscientization is a "permanent effort of man [*sic*] who seeks to situate himself [*sic*] in time and space, to exercise his [*sic*] creative potential, and to assume his [*sic*] responsibilities."[23]

Only after the oppressed are conscienticized can mutuality among them begin to develop. Though it is true that many of the oppressed do depend on other oppressed people to survive, frequently the oppressed do not see their common interests because they have to fight each other for the few crumbs that fall from the table of the oppressors. In many ways the oppressed depend for their survival on those who control the society in which they live — their oppressors. To even begin to envision the reality that is possible when they stand in solidarity with each other, the oppressed have to be willing to stop looking for and accepting the "charity" of their oppressors. To turn from the "charity" of the oppressors to solidarity among themselves requires great willingness to take risks. This going beyond the isolated self is followed by creating strategies to carry out their struggle for liberation. Implementing these strategies keeps hope alive and, together with the vision of their own liberation, gives the poor and oppressed the courage to risk that sustains the struggle.

Mutuality of the oppressor with the oppressed also starts with conscientization. To become aware that one is an oppressor does not stop with individual illumination but requires the oppressor to establish dialogue and mutuality with the oppressed.[24] The first word in the dialogue that can bring awareness to the oppressor is uttered by the oppressed. Oppressors who are willing to listen and to be questioned by the oppressed, by the very action of listening begin to leave behind their role as oppressors and to become "friends" of the oppressed.[25] This word spoken by the oppressed is "at times silent, at times muzzled; it is the face of the poor... of oppressed people who suffer violence."[26] This word is often spoken through demonstrations, boycotts, even revolutions. This word imposes itself "ethically, by a kind of categorical imperative, which is well determined and concrete, which the 'friend' as 'friend' listens to freely. This word... appeals to the 'friend's' domination and possession of the world and even of the other, and questions the desire for wealth and power."[27]

This word uttered by the oppressed divests those who allow themselves to be questioned by it of whatever they have totally appropriated. Although the word of the oppressed is seen as a weak word by the powerful, yet this "weak" word has the power to bring judgment. It judges the desire of the oppressor for wealth and power. It is also able to signify effectively the real possibility of liberation for those oppressors who allow themselves to be questioned. The word uttered by the oppressed is efficacious since, when listened to by oppressors, it enables them to make the qualitative jump that pushes them to become "friends," to establish mutuality with the oppressed. This word uttered by the oppressed gives the "friends" the courage to question and judge the structures that they have supported and from which they benefit, thus becoming co-creators with the oppressed of new liberating structures.

"Friends" answer the initial word of the oppressed not only by questioning their own lives but also by responding to the oppressed. Born of the critical consciousness acquired by allowing themselves to be critiqued and by taking responsibility for being oppressors, this response of the "friends" can help the oppressed in their own process of conscientization. Such response can help the oppressed to recognize the oppressor they carry within themselves and to rid themselves of him/her. The mutuality now established can help the oppressed to move away from seeking vengeance and from wanting to exchange places with the oppressors. This response of the "friends" can help the oppressed understand that they must not seek to participate in oppressive structures but rather to change those structures radically.[28]

If we do not recognize the need for the oppressed to learn from the "friends," then we cannot claim that mutuality is at the heart of solidarity. Solidarity requires a true dialogic relationship between oppressed and "friend." Our inability to embrace this mutuality, as described, has to do, I believe, with a romantic view of the oppressed which is sharply divorced from reality. If we fail to recognize that the "friends" need to do more than simply help the oppressed implement their strategies for liberation, no real mutuality, no real solidarity will exist. The process of conversion that becomes an intrinsic part of the lives of the "friends" makes it possible and necessary for them to question the oppressed about their goals. It makes it possible for the "friends" to participate with the oppressed in creating strategies for liberation, in deepening and clarifying the understanding of mutuality that is at the heart of liberation.

The "friends" of the oppressed are often scorned by those in whose circles they once moved because they threaten the powerful. The "friends," once oppressors themselves, know how to thwart control and domination. They are scorned because they know the manipulations and betrayals oppressors must make to stay in power and they can prick the consciences of their previous colleagues in ways the oppressed cannot. The "friends" are able to demystify the world of the oppressors, to expose its weakness and incoherence, to point out its lies.

However, at all times we must remember that it is the word uttered by the oppressed that starts and sustains the dialogic process of mutuality which stands at the heart of solidarity. We must not lose sight and begin to believe it is the "friends" who have initiated and now sustain the process of conscientization of the oppressor, a process that always has to be evolving. We also need to be conscious at all times that the "friends" as well as the oppressed derive their courage, their commitment to the struggle, and their staying power for the long run from a common vision of liberation.

Mutuality among the oppressed and between the oppressed and their "friends" is not simply a matter of reciprocal understanding and support, though that is or could be a very positive side effect. Mutuality as an element of solidarity must push the oppressed and their "friends" to revolutionary politics.[29] Mutuality urges them to envision and work toward alternative nonoppressive systems; otherwise they will not be able to sustain the revolutionary momentum that makes liberation possible.[30] Mutuality must push the oppressed and their "friends" to resist easy, partial solutions which may indeed alleviate oppression but not lead to liberation.

But this does not mean that we can wait until we have a perfect strategy or a perfect moment to act. No strategy is perfect. There are always internal problems and inconsistencies that need to be worked out. All strategies involve risk. This should never keep us from acting; it should never delay our work to try to establish mutuality, to create a community of solidarity committed to change oppressive structures, a community in which no one group of oppressed people will be sacrificed for the sake of another. This is what mutuality, the strategic component of solidarity, will accomplish.

Commitment to Mutuality

Solidarity will not become a reality unless we are totally committed to mutuality. As a matter of fact, I believe that commitment to mutuality is what makes it possible for the oppressed and their "friends" to maintain the revolutionary momentum of the struggle for liberation. Commitment to mutuality means "willingness to do something for or about whatever it is we are committed to (at least to protect it or affirm it when it is threatened)."[31] This is possible only if there is a "sense of being bound to whoever or whatever is the object of [this] commitment."[32] Commitment gives other persons or a worthy cause claim over oneself, thus establishing or strengthening mutuality between the self and the other. Commitment to mutuality results in "a relation of binding and being-bound, giving and being-claimed."[33]

Mutuality that has as its goal embracing commonality of interests demands commitment to action. Without action mutuality becomes a "soft word," a passing whimsical reaction which is often privatized and removed from the public sphere, from the political reality of the struggle for liberation. It is precisely the actions resulting from true commitment that are the framework of mutuality; they are the signs and deeds of mutuality and the efforts that ensure the future of mutuality.[34] It is these actions which express and constitute mutuality and which, in a limited but real way, begin to make liberation present. Actions born out of commitment to mutuality are "eschatological

glimpses" which clarify the vision of liberation that will become a reality in the kin-dom of God and which will make
faithfulness to the vision possible. Liberation is not a condition that already exists, simply waiting for the oppressed
to grasp it. Rather, liberation is a historical possibility that
takes form and shape according to the actions of the oppressed and their "friends." Liberative actions born out of
commitment to mutuality, therefore, are not only glimpses
of the future but eschatological actions making parts of the
future present now.

Commitment to mutuality is not a light or easy matter.
It involves all aspects of one's life and demands a lifelong
permanency. The way in which the commitment is lived
out may change. From time to time one may be less pas-
sionate about carrying out the implications of mutuality,
but somehow to go back and place oneself in a position of
control and domination over others is to betray mutuality,
to betray others and oneself. Such a betrayal, which most
of the time occurs by failing to engage in liberative praxis
rather than by formal denunciation, results in the "friends"
becoming oppressors once again and in the oppressed losing their vision of liberation. Betrayal, then, effectively
delays liberation and, therefore, at the very least makes
more difficult the unfolding of the kin-dom of God.[35]

Conclusion

More than two-thirds of the people in the world live under
terribly oppressive conditions. The way the gospel message to love our neighbor as we love ourselves has been
interpreted up to now leads the believer to the practice
of charity. But this interpretation does not help oppose
oppression; it is not an effective means to bring about

radical structural change in society. As we become aware of the alienation that oppression induces, we come to understand that love of neighbor is linked intrinsically and foremost to justice. In order for a person to become fully human, to overcome sin, to move from alienation to a love-relationship with God and with others, justice has to prevail. "As virtue, justice is a trait of character empowering and disposing an agent to act in ways constitutive of human flourishing."[36] This is why the unfolding of the kin-dom of God, which indeed promotes human fulfillment, is made possible only when just structures and situations exist. "This is the reason why the effort to build a just society is liberating."[37] This is why "action on behalf of justice and transformation of the world fully appear...as a constitutive element of the preaching of the Gospel."[38] And, finally, this is why Christianity can be reaffirmed as containing truth, "not because of its origins, but because it liberates people now from specific forms of oppression."[39]

Understanding the centrality of justice has led us to look at other ways of implementing the command to love our neighbors that do not stop with giving. We have come to appreciate the need for radical structural change and the fact that unless we recognize the interdependence of all persons, we face a very bleak future. But recognition of interdependence will not happen apart from a sense of commonality of interest, which in turn will lead us to discover solidarity with the poor and the oppressed and with those committed to justice. Solidarity, then, is a virtue. It is an attitude and disposition that greatly influences how we act. As a virtue solidarity becomes a way of life. It becomes the new way of living out "the love your neighbor as yourself" that up to now has been interpreted as giving out of our largesse. Given the network of oppressive structures in our world today that so control and dominate the vast majority of human beings, the only way we can continue to claim the centrality of love of neighbor for Christians is to redefine what it means and what it demands of us. Solidarity, then, becomes the new way of understanding and living out this commandment of the gospel.

Notes

1. Originally I dedicated this essay to Blanche Marie Moore, a sister in the Order of St. Ursula who died in the Bronx, New York, on December 10, 1987, as I was writing it. Today I rededicate it to her. Blanche Marie was my high school teacher in Cuba. A person of great strength of character, her dedication and strong will caught my imagination and strongly influenced me. I will always be most grateful to her for imbuing in me a love of reading and studying. *In paradisum perducant te angeli*, Blanche.

2. One year, as his birthday approached, Cáceres came to ask if he could connect an electric wire to our house. He strung it across the street and into his house, providing light so he could party all night long. Knowing we would not sleep at all that night, the eight women of our household settled to listen to the music Cáceres and his friends created, loud singing and banging on pots and pans well into the night. When I left Perú I gave Cáceres my bongos as a token of appreciation for all he had taught me.

3. Just in case we have forgotten, the Contras were an armed, illegal group, heavily supported by the USA, which fought to overturn the Sandinista government, a freely elected, legally constituted government.

4. My concern is similar to that of Paulo Freire many years ago about the use/misuse of the word "conscientization." He stopped using the word; I am choosing to work hard at returning its original meaning to "solidarity."

5. See Isabel Carter Heyward, *The Redemption of God* (Lanham, Md.: University Press of America, 1982), 1–18.

6. In this essay the terms "the poor" and "the oppressed" are at times used interchangeably and at times together. I would have preferred to use the term "nonperson" — those human beings who are considered less than human by societies based on privileges arrogated by a minority (Gustavo Gutiérrez, *The Power of the Poor in History* [Maryknoll, N.Y.: Orbis Books, 1984], 92). But I am concerned that the ontological meaning of "nonentity" would be read into my use of "nonperson," regardless of the explanation provided. I thought of using only "the oppressed" but felt that "the oppressed" could be seen as a classification, an abstraction, instead of concrete persons.

I then needed to decide what term to add to "the oppressed." I thought of the term I use to identify my own oppression, "Hispanic women," but felt that it was too specific and that what I say here could be understood to apply only to us. I decided to use "the poor" because, though the restricted meaning of the term relates to those who are economically oppressed, it often goes beyond that meaning and closely parallels the meaning of the oppressed even in everyday language. In the Bible, at least in the book of Zephaniah 2:3, 3:12–13, "the poor" are identified with the *anawim*. The *anawim*, the poor, are "the portion of the community...upon which the possible future existence of the community depends (E. Jenni, "Remnant," *The Interpreter's Dictionary of the Bible*, ed. George Arthur Buttrick [Nashville: Abingdon, 1965], 32–33). My usage of "the poor" in this chapter definitely includes this meaning.

7. *The Random House Dictionary of the English Language*, 2nd unabridged ed. (New York: Random House, 1987).

8. There are two reasons for not using the regular word employed by English Bibles "kingdom." First, it is obviously a sexist word that presumes that God is male. Second, the concept of kingdom in our world today is both hierarchical and elitist — as is the word "reign." The word "kin-dom" makes it clear that when the fullness of God becomes a day-to-day reality in the world at large, we will all be sisters and brothers — kin to each other; we will indeed be the family of God.

9. Gustavo Gutiérrez, *A Theology of Liberation* (Maryknoll, N.Y.: Orbis Books, 1973), 159.

10. Ibid., 177.

11. Rebecca S. Chopp, *Praxis of Suffering* (Maryknoll, N.Y.: Orbis Books, 1986), 25.

12. Gutiérrez, *A Theology of Liberation*, 175.

13. José Míguez Bonino, "Nueva tendencias en teología," *Pasos* no. 9 (1987): 22.

14. Gutiérrez, *The Power of the Poor in History*, 140.

15. Ibid.

16. Gutiérrez, *A Theology of Liberation*, 289.

17. I use these three "isms" as inclusive categories and paradigms of oppression. Under sexism, for example, I include heterosexism. Under classism I include militarism, etc.

18. I use "strategy" instead of "practice" here because of my insistence on the intrinsic unity between reflection and practice. I also use "strategy" because it carries with it the implication of political effectiveness which is intrinsic to solidarity as a praxis of liberation.

19. Janice Raymond, *A Passion for Friends* (Boston: Beacon Press, 1986), 22.

20. Ibid., 214–15.

21. Gutiérrez, *A Theology of Liberation*, 92.

22. Paulo Freire, *Pedagogy of the Oppressed* (New York: Seabury Press, 1973), 3.

23. Gutiérrez, *A Theology of Liberation*, 92.

24. I have based this section about the relationship between the oppressor and the "friend" on Juan Carlos Scannone, *Teología de la liberación y praxis popular* (Salamanca: Ediciones Sígueme, 1976), 133–86.

25. Scannone uses the word "brother." I have used "friend" in translating into English in order to avoid a sexist term.

26. Ibid.

27. Scannone, *Teología de la liberación y praxis popular*, 164. In translating I have used inclusive language even though the original does not.

28. Karen Lebacqz, *Justice in an Unjust World* (Minneapolis: Fortress Press, 1987), 110–11.

29. bell hooks, *Feminist Theory: From Margin to Center* (Boston: South End Press, 1984), 159.

30. Ibid.

31. Margaret Farley, *Personal Commitments* (San Francisco: Harper & Row, 1986), 14.

32. Ibid., 15.

33. Ibid., 18–19.

34. See Farley, *Personal Commitments*, 36.

35. I find Gutiérrez wavering when he comes to this issue of the relationship between liberation and the kin-dom of God. In *A Theology of Liberation* he says, "it is only in the temporal, earthly, historical event that we can open up to the future complete fulfillment" (167). But Gutiérrez later insists on a different understanding: "nor does it mean that this just society constitutes a 'necessary condition' for the arrival of the Kingdom, nor that they are closely linked, nor that they converge" (231). I too waver on this issue. Does betrayal of mutuality, because it delays liberation, impede or merely make it more difficult for the kin-dom of God to unfold?

36. William Werpehowski, "Justice," in James F. Childress and John Macquarrie, eds., *The Westminster Dictionary of Christian Ethics* (Philadelphia: Westminster Press, 1986), 338.

37. Gutiérrez, *A Theology of Liberation*, 177.

38. Synod of Bishops Second General Assembly, November 30, 1971, "Justice in the World," in Joseph Gremillion, ed., *The Gospel of Peace and Justice* (Maryknoll, N.Y.: Orbis Books, 1976), 514.

39. Sharon D. Welch, *Communities of Resistance and Solidarity* (Maryknoll, N.Y.: Orbis Books, 1985), 53.

Un Poquito de Justicia
A Little Bit of Justice

The president of the Madres Cristianas — Christian Mothers — group of the parish where I worship on weekends in New York City on weekends called me early in February. She was inviting me to plan and lead a *servicio de la amistad* — a friendship service — at her house. After all, she could not let the month of St. Valentine's go by without gathering friends and celebrating something so important as friendship. I was happy to accept the invitation and to be present on a Sunday afternoon with about fifteen others (all but three were women) to celebrate friendship and community. During the service we had an opportunity to share what it is that we expect from friends and what we have to offer to friends. Later, we ate together, talked endlessly about the islands where we were born, and reminisced about customs of our birth-lands that had been very important for us since our youth. We lamented, too, the loss of certain cultural practices instrumental in teaching us about ourselves and about life, which have served as

---

An earlier version of this essay, entitled "*Un Poquito de Justicia* — A Little Bit of Justice: A *Mujerista* Account of Justice," was published in Ada María Isasi-Díaz and Fernando F. Segovia, eds., *Hispanic/Latino Theology: Challenge and Promise* (Minneapolis: Fortress, 1996), pp. 325–39. Reprinted with permission. Copyright © 1996 Augsburg Fortress.

resources for our survival as a minority culture within the United States.

As story after story was shared, it became very obvious that these women (the men were mostly silent or talked among themselves), had lived many times the "no greater love" message of Jesus recorded in the Gospel of John read during the *servicio de la amistad*. The women's theological understanding of this central text of Christianity is revealed not in elaborated discourse but rather in thought-full implementation. For them "no greater love" is *not* a matter of dying for someone else but a matter of not allowing someone else to die. For them "no greater love" is a matter of taking in children who are not necessarily blood relatives but whose parents cannot provide for them. For them "no greater love" is a matter of worrying about their neighborhood instead of worrying about ways of making it out of the neighborhood. For them "no greater love" has to do with *un poquito de justicia* — a little bit of justice — that they think society owes the Latino community so "at least our children can have a fighting chance to survive the drug war." For them "no greater love" is nothing but the justice-demand that is a constitutive element of the gospel message.

Latinas' Cries: Starting Point for Understanding Justice

As is true of all our theological work, the reason for articulating a *mujerista* perspective of justice is to contribute to the struggle for liberation of Latinas, which cannot happen apart from the liberation of all Hispanics and all oppressed people. Our goal is to do away with injustice, to create spaces for justice to flourish so that the unfolding of the kin-dom[1] of God can become a reality in our lives, in our society. And where are we to start?

Mujerista theology has consistently insisted on the lived-experience of Latinas as not only the *locus theologicus,* the starting place of theological reflection, but the very source of our theology.[2] It is not surprising then that as *mujerista* theology attempts to articulate an understanding of justice, our starting point is the cries against injustice of grassroots Latinas who struggle daily to survive.

We have insisted on lived-experience of Latinas as the source of *mujerista* theology because we believe in the on-going revelation of God in our lives. Further, we certainly believe that fidelity to the gospel message requires us to have a preferential option for the poor and the oppressed. A third reason has to do with the commitment of *mujerista* theology to provide a platform for the voices of grassroots Latinas. Providing Latinas with opportunities to articulate their understandings of religious beliefs and practices is a consciousness-raising enterprise and, as such, it is a liberative strategy.

Consciousness-raising from a *mujerista* theology perspective has to do with sharing understandings about beliefs and practices that are oppressive for Latinas. The sharing — putting in common — of religious beliefs that oppress us helps Latinas to know that they are not mistaken in rejecting such beliefs, that they are not alone in thinking that "there is really no way God makes that happen, or permits it, or requires that of us." By sharing their beliefs Latinas begin to understand how religion has been used to control them, to silence them, to keep them submissive. Sharing often helps them see clearly that what they say they believe is not always what they "really believe." Group theological reflection makes it possible for the real religious beliefs and understandings of Latinas to come to the surface, to be articulated. And those true nonconscious religious beliefs, although often suppressed, are many times the real source of these women's strength as they struggle for survival *día a día* — day in and day out.

A fourth reason for using the lived-experience of Latinas as the source of *mujerista* theology, of listening to the cries of Latinas as the starting point for an elaboration of justice, has to do with the demand that the gospel message makes on all Christians to stand in solidarity with the poor and the oppressed.[3] To stand in solidarity with the poor and the oppressed one has to start by listening to their cries. Solidarity is a response to the cry for justice of those who are victimized. Those who are non-poor or less poor, non-oppressed or less oppressed, are not capable of deciding on their own to be in solidarity with those who suffer oppression. Because the preferential option for the poor and the oppressed is based on the gospel message found in Matthew 25:31–46, we can assert that the "grace of conversion" is given as we listen to what the oppressed have to say and as we discover how we ourselves are involved in and profit from their oppression.

Five Modes of Oppression

What is injustice? What is oppression? Elsewhere we have explored the particulars of the oppression suffered by Latinas.[4] Here we will continue to examine the nature of this oppression because it is the starting point in the struggle for justice, which is the goal of our theological practice. We approach justice by examining the structures of oppression that force Latinas to live in the midst of unjust structures. *Mujeristas'* understanding of justice, therefore, is not based on philosophical speculations regarding what criteria to apply in determining what is due to Latinas. Justice for us refers not only to what we receive but also to our active and effective participation in making justice a reality. "A just social order cannot be created for the poor nor can it be created without them. It needs their active participation at all levels of the struggle and our committed solidarity with them."[5]

Injustice causes the poor and oppressed to suffer "inhibition of their ability to develop and exercise their capacities and express their needs, thoughts, and feelings."[6] Injustice, however, is not only a matter of personal suffering caused by given individuals.

> Oppression also refers to systemic constraints.... Its causes are embedded in unquestioned norms, habits, and symbols, in the assumptions underlying institutional rules and the collective consequences of following those rules.... Oppression refers to the vast and deep injustices some groups suffer as a consequence of often unconscious assumptions and reactions of well-meaning people in ordinary interactions, media and cultural stereotypes, and structural features of bureaucratic hierarchies and market mechanisms — in short, the normal processes of everyday life.[7]

There are different reasons, or combinations of reasons, for the oppression Latinas suffer. Therefore it is not possible to give one definition of our oppression or, indeed, of any oppression. We do well in our analysis of oppression to look at different modes of oppression operative in people's daily lives, in *lo cotidiano*. Certainly there is no moral primacy among the causes or factors or elements of oppression: there is no one kind of oppression that is worse than another, no one face of oppression that is more oppressive than another. Often we suffer oppression one way while we oppress others in another way. Differentiating the modes of oppression, however, does help us to grasp the dynamics of oppression and this, we hope, will help in the development of strategies in the work for justice.[8]

Exploitation is one mode of oppression. It has to do with processes that transfer the results of the labor of Latinas to benefit others. When we talk about exploitation we are talking about what work is, who does what for whom, how work is compensated, and how and by whom the result of that work is appropriated. The energy of Latinas is "continuously expended to maintain and augment the power, status, and wealth of the haves."[9]

The fact that, in general, Latinas' wages are below those of Euro-Americans and Latino men is one sign of exploitation. The fact that Latinas in factories around the United States are paid according to what they produce instead of according to the amount of time they work is a matter of exploitation. But exploitation of Latinas has to do not only with their labor in factories, industrial plants, and other economic institutions of society. Latinas also suffer gender exploitation. In their homes Latinas work for their men. Latinas are, most of the time, responsible for *lo cotidiano:* keeping house for their husbands or male partners; "finding" the economic resources needed to keep a roof over their own heads as well as those of their children and male partners, to provide for the food and medical expenses of the family. Latinas also are responsible for providing for the emotional needs not only of the children in the family but of the husband, father, and brothers.

Moreover, Latinas suffer exploitation in the churches. They do much of the work while the priests or pastors take credit for it. Latinas are the economic backbone of most of the churches but they are not allowed to participate —

never fully, seldom partially — in the decisions of how the monies they work so hard to collect are to be spent. Latinas are the ones in charge of cleaning the churches, making and setting up decorations for Holy Week and Easter, for example; Latinas are, to a large extent, the ones responsible for bringing men and children to church. But their work is not recognized, nor is it compensated. Instead it is appropriated by the men who control what happens in the churches. For example, in many churches Latinas are not included among the twelve who get their feet washed by the pastor during the Holy Thursday celebration; in many other parishes they are included only after long and bitter arguments with the priests year after year. Considering all that Latinas contribute to make Holy Thursday celebrations meaningful for their communities, their exclusion from leadership roles in the celebration itself is exploitation.

The second face of oppression is that of marginalization. This is perhaps the most dangerous form of oppression: as marginalized people Latinas are part of a category of people who are not seen as contributing to society and, therefore, are subject to severe material deprivation and even extermination. The marginalized are surplus people who not only are considered to be useless by others but come to understand themselves that way as well. Marginalization "involves the deprivation of cultural, practical, and institutionalized conditions for exercising capacities in a context of recognition and interaction."[10] All this leads to lack of self-respect, to identity crisis, to lack of self-worth, to *un hastío* — a disgusting boredom — that is totally destructive. It is not surprising, then, that in different areas of the country Latinas are increasingly among those who abuse alcohol and drugs.

Latina women are marginalized by the dominant culture

and within it, but patriarchal understandings and structures also marginalize us within our own communities. I have heard so many times in different meetings and gatherings of Latinos and Latinas, "Aquí las mujeres no tienen nada que decir" ("here the women have nothing to say"). And, even when we are discounted, when we are marginalized, I marvel at the faithfulness of grassroots Latinas to our communities. At those same meetings when some Latinas have tried to disagree with Latinos conducting the meeting and have been ignored, I have seen the Latinas sign up to carry out whatever has been decided.

Powerlessness is a third face of oppression. As powerless persons Latinas lack authority. Power is exercised over us: we are to do what we are told; we have little or no autonomy, little or no opportunity to be self-defining, to assert our interests and visions of what we believe is good for our communities. As powerless persons Latinas lack status, are not considered respectable. Latinas cannot presume, as others in the society do, that they will be trusted and respected unless they do something to forfeit that trust or respect. Latinas know that we have to earn trust, that we have to earn respect and that we have to keep earning it or we will not have it.

This is true even of those of us who are professionals, who have earned high academic degrees and hold positions of regard. As a Latina professor of theology I can fill several pages with stories of the demands students make of me, with the negative attitude some have toward me, with their lack of respect for my authority.[11] I must confess that I have been slow to recognize this. It has been my women colleagues who have pointed out to me that the same students who have disregarded my critiques and evaluations have accepted without question similar decisions about the quality of their work from other professors. And if this is so for professionals, how much more difficult is it for grassroots Latinas?

Because powerlessness results in lack of autonomy, powerlessness makes it extremely difficult for Latinas to exercise their creativity. *Si yo pudiera* — if only I could — that is the repeated cry of Latinas who have very few, if any, avenues for developing and expressing their creativity. It seems that only in the role of mothers can Latinas find some space to be creative. But then, whatever creativity Latinas might have in the way they nurture and educate their children is seriously curtailed by the expectations society has of motherhood and also by the imperative need Latinas have to teach their children how to survive. How can we teach our children to be free if we have to keep them inside the house so they will not be shot to death? How can we teach our children to ask questions, to dream dreams and see visions, when we know that to survive one has to comply?

The fourth face of oppression is cultural imperialism, the very basis for ethnic prejudice and racism. To experience cultural imperialism is to experience how the dominant meanings of a society render our particular Latina perspectives invisible. It means to be stereotyped precisely as "other," as "outsider." Cultural imperialism in its concrete form of ethnic and gender-based prejudice against Latinas means that the experience and culture of non-Latinas are the norm in this society. Non-Latinas "project their own experience as representative of humanity as such,"[12] and our own experience is constructed largely as deviant and inferior.

The culturally dominated undergo a paradoxical oppression, in that they are both marked by stereotypes and at the same time rendered invisible. As remark-

able, deviant being, the culturally imperialized are
stamped with an essence. The stereotypes confine
them to a nature which is often attached in some way
to their bodies, and which thus cannot easily be denied. These stereotypes so permeate the society that
they are not noticed as contestable.[13]

But the most destructive aspect of cultural imperialism — of ethnic prejudice and racism — is not what it does
to Latinas but what it makes Latinas do to our own selves.
Little by little we internalize the way the dominant culture sees us — when it sees us — for we are always obliged
to act according to the image society has of us. Little by
little our own culture and our self-understandings become
as invisible to ourselves as they are to the dominant culture. And that invisibility finds expression in a rejection
of our cultural customs and values, in a rejection of ourselves as Latinas that is all the more insidious because
of how imperceptible it is, even — perhaps mainly — to
ourselves.[14]

The fifth face of oppression is systemic violence. Latinas
live with the fear of random, unprovoked attacks on their
persons or property which have no motive but to damage,
humiliate, or destroy them. What makes the violence Latinas suffer a face of oppression is not the particular acts —
no matter how horrible they are — but the fact that there
is a societal context that makes such actions possible and
acceptable. This is why the police, for example, feel free
to treat grassroots Latinas with violence, something they,
in general, are less likely to do to Euro-American women,
and much less to middle-class Euro-American men. And
what about domestic violence, a pervasive crime Latinas of
all economic strata repeatedly suffer? The *no te metas* — do
not interfere — response to domestic violence makes it ob-

vious that this kind of violence is acceptable to society at large and to our own Latino communities.

But what perhaps makes violence such a destructive force of oppression is that the suffering violence inflicts, both physically and psychologically, is so devastating and all-encompassing, that the possibility of such violence becomes an ever-present threat coercing us day in and day out. The possibility of displeasing her male partner who will show his displeasure by beating her, for example, will keep a Latina from going to women's meetings — relating to church or community matters — where she is appreciated and needed. The fear of rape, the number one form of violence against Latinas and all women in the USA, is such a threat to us that many Latinas live very restricted lives as a means of self-protection. The insidiousness of violence, then, is that it becomes a threat, and threats are economic means of coercion: they get Latinas to do what they do not choose to do without the oppressor having to actually spend any energy, without the oppressor having to do anything.[15]

A *Mujerista* Account of Justice

The reason for taking time to study oppression is to find effective means of working against it and for justice. The reason for articulating a *mujerista* understanding of justice is to bring about justice. Being a liberative praxis, *mujerista* theology has to be effective, in this case contributing to the elimination of injustice. This means that our understanding of justice has to be precise enough to force an option.[16] Elsewhere I have sought to spell out particulars of a *mujerista* vision of justice by describing Latinas' *proyecto histórico* — our preferred future.[17] Here, starting from the injustice Latinas suffer and keeping our eyes firmly fixed

on what we see as conditions for and of the kin-dom of
God — our vision of justice — I try to make explicit some
principles of justice that embrace and reveal Latinas' expectations regarding a just world order. The elements of
justice presented here are not a theory of justice in the
classical sense. That is, they do not constitute a construct
that applies "to all or most societies, whatever their concrete configuration and social relations, from a few general
premises about the nature of human beings, the nature
of societies, and the nature of reason."[18] I refer here to a
mujerista "account" of justice instead of to a *mujerista* "theory" of justice. But the elements of this account, I believe,
must be included in all accounts of justice. How the elements are understood, what is their concrete and historic
content, may vary, but the following elements should be
present.

The first element of a *mujerista* account of justice has
to do with its goal: establishing justice rather than building
a systematic theory. The liberative praxis of Latinas to establish justice starts by claiming an intrinsic union between
practice and reflection. Praxis is not to be understood as
action apart from reflection but rather refers to reflective
action. However, a *mujerista* account of justice does not
avoid rational thinking. Latinas' liberative praxis is not a
doing without a thinking.[19] The thinking and reflecting,
the analysis and arguments that are part of Latinas' liberative praxis clarify the meaning of ideas and issues, describe
the relations among ourselves and between Latinas and society at large, and make clear our vision — our ideals and
principles. Because the aim of a *mujerista* account of justice is not correct articulation (though it does not exclude
it) but effective justice-seeking praxis, our account of justice is a process that reflects the ever changing reality of
Latinas.[20]

The second element of a *mujerista* account of justice refers to its concreteness, to its contextualization: it has to be concrete, and, therefore, it has to be historical. This is why a *mujerista* account of justice begins with injustice: that is the reality the vast majority of Latinas live today. Our account of justice does not depend on philosophical reasoning but on the stories of oppression Latinas tell.[21] The role those stories play in elaborating a *mujerista* account of justice builds on and supports the contention that we must construct our articulation of justice from within the struggle for justice, from the perspective of injustice. This means that we need good social, political, and economic descriptions and analyses of Latinas' reality, always keeping in mind that our descriptions and explanations have to be critical; they have to evaluate and point to liberation.[22]

The third element of a *mujerista* account of justice is the other side of the previous one: our account of justice points to a discontinuity — some discontinuity, *not* total discontinuity — with our past and present reality. This means that justice "is not dependent on the possibilities inherent in the past."[23] This discontinuity is based on the role that the realization of the kin-dom of God plays in Latinas' *proyecto histórico* — historical project.[24] In *mujerista* theology history is one; there are not two histories, a secular one and a sacred one. The history of salvation — the realization of the kin-dom of God — does not happen apart from the daily struggles of Latinas to survive. "Without liberating historical events, there would be no growth of the Kingdom [*sic*]. But the process of liberation will not have conquered the very roots of human oppression and exploitation without the coming of the Kingdom [*sic*], which is above all a gift."[25] But though the kin-dom is a gift of God, it also "requires certain behaviors from those who receive it. It is *already* present in history, *but* it does not reach its complete fulfillment therein. Its presence already produces effects, but these are not *the* coming of the Kingdom [*sic*], not *all* of salvation; they are anticipations of a completion that will be realized only beyond human history."[26]

The fourth element of a *mujerista* account of justice has to do with recognizing and dealing with differences rather than just acknowledging the "problem" of differences.[27] This means that justice has to move beyond acceptance that there are different ways of being to real interaction. Interaction between those who are different is not possible unless one recognizes how cultural imperialism functions in the United States, how those who do not belong to the dominant group are conceptualized as other, as inferior and deviant.[28] Interaction among Latinas and non-Latinas will lead to participation and inclusion in a way that does not require us to renounce who we are. Interaction leads to opportunities for Latinas to make their own contribution to what is normative in society, to have a *papel pro-tagónico* — protagonist role — in society. To recognize and deal with differences, to embrace differences, is to reject assimilation, to reject an essentialist meaning of difference that places groups and persons in categorical opposition, in mutual exclusion.[29] To embrace differences means to understand differences as "ambiguous, relational, shifting, without clear borders that keep people straight — as entail-ing neither amorphous unity nor pure individuality."[30] To embrace differences means to insist on the specificity of Latinas as relational rather than as a substantive category or unequivocal attributes.

A relational understanding of group difference rejects exclusion. Difference no longer implies that groups lie outside one another. To say that there are differences among groups does not imply that there are not over-lapping experiences, or that two groups have nothing in common. The assumption that real differences in affinity, culture, or privilege imply oppositional categorization must be challenged. Different groups are always similar in some respects, and always potentially share some attributes, experiences, and goals.[31]

Because embracing differences requires interaction and because interaction cannot happen without honest dialogue (which in turn requires equalization of power among those dialoguing), the fifth element of a *mujerista* account of justice has to deal with power. A *mujerista* understanding of power, like our account of justice, starts from the underside of history, from those who are powerless. Power, therefore, has to be understood both as a personal and as a structural process that can be used for oppression or liberation. Oppressive power uses force, coercion, and/or influence to control, to limit, the self-determination and decision-making of individual persons or groups of persons.[32] Liberative power is used to transform oppressive situations, situations of domination. In a liberative use of power a

dominant agent...exercises power over a subordinate agent for the latter's benefit....However, the dominant agent's aim is not simply to act for the benefit of the subordinate agent; rather the dominant agent attempts to exercise his power in such a way that the subordinate agent learns certain skills that undercut the power differential between her and the dominant agent. The...[liberative] use of power is a use of power that seeks to bring about its own obsolescence by means of the empowerment of the subordinate.[33]

Two points need to be clarified here. First, in a liberative use of power, the learning of skills by the subordinate agent is a matter of taking power, of becoming self-defining and self-actualizing. It is precisely because of this that the power of the dominant agent becomes obsolescent, non-operative. Second, the word "empowerment" can indeed be read to mean that power is given, not taken. My contention here is that liberative power is exercised within the context of a relationship, of a give-and-take between dominant and subordinate agent in which not all the giving is done by the dominant and not all the taking by the subordinate but in which both agents give and take. It is my contention that the kind of relationship needed for the development of a relationship — for the presence of liberative power — has to be one of solidarity between those who have power and those who are powerless.

The process of solidarity, like the process of power and of justice, starts with the cry of the oppressed, with the oppressor listening intently to what the oppressed have to say. This listening requires and at the same time results in vulnerability on the part of the powerful, an attitude that will lead them to understand how they benefit from oppressive structures and how they contribute to the oppression of those whose cries are awakening them to their own injustice. This is all part of a process of conversion that results in the oppressor being in solidarity with the oppressed, in using his/her privileges to undo oppressive structures. The oppressor has now become "friend" and has to establish a dialogic relationship — a relationship of mutuality — with the oppressed. It is within this relationship of mutuality that both the dominant and the subordinate agents empower each other, that liberative power is exercised.[34]

The sixth element of a *mujerista* articulation of justice is the Latinas' belief that justice cannot be achieved at the expense of justice for others.[35] Therefore, we reject theories of justice such as utilitarianism and the liberal understanding of entitlements, which are in many ways responsible for the present USA meritocratic society in which the main concern is to be sure everyone has an equality of opportunity to release one's "energies in the pursuit of economic prosperity and political domination."[36] Believing that no one is expendable, our *mujerista* account of justice "requires redistribution from those who are better off to those who are worse off until that point after which further redistribution no longer increases the long-term absolute size of the shares of those who are worse off."[37]

But a *mujerista* account of justice goes beyond redistribution and calls for restitution.[38] It does so not with a spirit of vengeance, to get even. It does so not out of a sense that we have a right to receive back what was taken from our communities and nations of origin, for we demand restitution on behalf of what we need for justice to exist and flourish now and in the future and not in view of what we had in the past.[39] Restitution has to do with equalizing power. This means that redistribution cannot be understood by rich and powerful as an injustice and by the poor and oppressed — by Latinas — as a handout. Without some restitution, without some equalization of power, Latinas will not be able to capitalize on what they receive through any form of redistribution. This means that Latinas and other poor and oppressed people will always be in the position of having to demand redistribution, and our lives will continue to be controlled and limited by the rich and powerful. Without some operative sense of restitution we will not have a society where all have access to what they need to be creative, self-defining persons, who participate in setting what is normative for society and who have the opportunity to share in societal goods. Redistribution that includes restitution will result in "mutual benefits" that expresses "a conception of reciprocity,"[40] which is an intrinsic element of the mutuality we see as central to a *mujerista* account of justice.

The seventh element of a *mujerista* account of justice is the insistence at all times that Latinas' rights are both socioeconomic rights — having to do with restitution and redistribution — as well as civic-political rights. Justice has to do with the right we have to food, adequate housing, health care, and access to the fertility of the earth, to the productivity of industrialized society, and to the benefits provided by social security. For us justice also has to do with freedom of religion, expression, and assembly, due process of the law, participation in the creation of social and political structures, and participation in the leadership and government of such structures in a much more direct way than is at present provided in the "representative form" used in the USA.[41]

At first glance this proposal having to do with rights could be seen as being quite the same as the classical, liberal agenda of justice. However, it seems to me that there are four important considerations to be made before this judgment is passed on our proposal. First, as the first element of this *mujerista* account of justice makes clear, we see this account as a process, a first moment in the process. If we keep this in mind, the insistence on these two kinds of rights as a starting place for the Latinas' struggle for justice for ourselves and our communities is a logical place to start. Second, by itself this element of our account of justice might not seem radical, but taking it together with the other elements of this *mujerista* account I believe makes it very radical. Just think of the radicalness of claiming socioeconomic and civil-political rights when part of the claim would include a new way of understanding and dealing with power as well as a redistribution of wealth and privileges coupled with restitution. Third, this call for recognition and granting of rights to Latinas is coupled in this account with a radically different understanding about differences than the prevalent one of equality. This means that the claiming of rights is not so that Latinas can be assimilated into society but rather so that Latinas and our communities can be an intrinsic part of the USA society without losing our specificity. For that to happen a radical change as to how this society understands itself has to take place. Finally, in emphasizing both socioeconomic as well as civic-political rights, this *mujerista* account of justice makes it clear that considerations of social justice — what are considered by some to be macro issues — cannot be articulated apart from personal justice — usually classified as micro issues — and, therefore, considered by many liberals as unimportant. As *mujeristas* we hold to the dictum that "the personal is political" and that the separation of the so-called private from the public sector has played a significant role in our oppression as women.

The eighth and final element of a *mujerista* account of justice brings us back to a passing comment made earlier: our account of justice has to be useful; it has to be effective. In order to be so, a *mujerista* account of justice has to help Latinas to understand our world, to locate ourselves concretely in it, and to see the role we play in maintaining such a world. Our account of justice has to denounce injustice, but it also has to indicate modes of resistance instead of encouraging complicity with injustice.[42] A *mujerista* account of justice, we repeat, has to announce our *proyecto histórico* in a precise enough way so as to make choosing necessary, so as to force an option against injustice and for justice.

"No Greater Love": A Matter of Justice

That Sunday afternoon of the *servicio de la amistad* I understood better than ever what I had read years before: "One of the most disastrous errors in the history of Christianity is to have tried — under the influence of Greek definitions — to differentiate between love and justice."[43] This was exactly what we had been saying all afternoon and into the evening as we shared stories about our lives and our *añoranzas* — nostalgic yearnings. By early evening I was once again in awe at the depth of theological understanding of these grassroots Latinas.

I am convinced that these women live Anselm's definition of theology: "faith seeking understanding." Their religious practices — devotional practices such as praying the rosary, praying to the saints, and making offerings at their home altars as well as the way Latinas daily bring their religious understandings to bear on what we do, on the decisions we make — are not unreflected customs performed automatically. Mostly we learned our religious practices from our mothers, our aunts, and our grandmothers. As we watched these older women, Latinas learned not only these religious practices but also their meaning. Together with the manner of performing these practices we learned that these practices were to sustain our lives, were to give us *fuerzas para la lucha* — strength for the struggle. These practices were to be in many instances *los medios para la lucha* — the means for the struggle.

I drove home that Sunday evening reaffirming my conviction that the women with whom I had shared several hours are *mujerista* theologians. They can indeed give us a clear understanding of who God is, how we touch the divine in our daily lives, how we live the gospel message of justice and peace.

Notes

1. I do not use "kingdom" because it is obviously a sexist word that presumes that God is male. Second, the concept of kingdom in our world today is both hierarchical and elitist, which is also why I do not use "reign." The word "kin-dom" makes it clear that when the fullness of God becomes a day-to-day reality in our world, we will all be kin to each other.

2. See Ada María Isasi-Díaz and Yolanda Tarango, *Hispanic Women: Prophetic Voice in the Church* (San Francisco: Harper and Row, 1988; reprint Minneapolis: Fortress Press, 1992); Ada María Isasi-Díaz, *En la Lucha — Elaborating a Mujerista Theology* (Minneapolis: Fortress Press, 1993).

3. I have dealt with the issue of solidarity at length in "Solidarity: Love of Neighbor in the Twenty-First Century," included in the present volume, pp. 86–104.

4. Isasi-Díaz and Tarango, *Hispanic Women;* Isasi-Díaz, *En la Lucha,* chapters 1 and 2.

5. Ismael García, *Justice in Latin American Theology of Liberation* (Atlanta: John Knox Press, 1982), 82.

6. Iris Marion Young, *Justice and the Politics of Difference* (Princeton, N.J.: Princeton University Press, 1990), 40.

7. Ibid., 41.

8. The analysis of oppression that follows is based on the one presented and explored by Iris Marion Young in *Justice and the Politics of Difference,* chapter 6.

9. Ibid., 50.

10. Ibid., 55.

11. Of course I could retaliate against those students by giving them low grades. But, first, I believe that would be unethical. Second, though I try to do what I believe I should do as a professor, the fact that the evaluation of courses students submit to the dean play a role in my reviews certainly makes me put up with behavior from students that I find objectionable. The point I am making here, however, is that this attitude toward me of some students — enough to be noticed though by no means a great number — creates an atmosphere around me and about me that results in weakening my authority and power not only with the students but also with the institution at large.

12. Ibid., 59.

13. Ibid.

14. María C. Lugones, "On the Logic of Pluralist Feminism," in Claudia Card, ed., *Feminist Ethics* (Lawrence: University Press of Kansas, 1991), 35–44; Young, *Justice and the Politics of Difference,* 60.

15. For a comprehensive analysis of force, threat, and coercion as el-

ements of oppression see Thomas E. Wartenberg, *The Forms of Power* (Philadelphia: Temple University Press, 1990), 91–104.

16. For a fuller treatment of this issue see Isasi-Díaz, *En la Lucha*, 34–45.

17. Ibid.

18. Young, *Justice and the Politics of Difference*, 3.

19. See Isasi-Díaz and Tarango, *Hispanic Women*, chapter 1, for a wider discussion of this point.

20. This does not mean that we embrace relativism, though we do indeed accept a certain amount of relativity as a given. Process and change are here to be seen as parts of development, of growth, but within the definitiveness that liberation as the goal of justice indicates.

21. Karen Lebacqz, *Justice in an Unjust World* (Minneapolis: Augsburg Publishing House, 1987), 150–51.

22. Young, *Justice and the Politics of Difference*, 5.

23. Lebacqz, *Justice in an Unjust World*, 153.

24. This claim to a discontinuity between what is and what justice will be is also based on the epistemological privilege of the poor and the oppressed that we claim for Latinas and to which we referred above.

25. Gustavo Gutiérrez, *A Theology of Liberation*, 2d ed. (Maryknoll, N.Y.: Orbis Books, 1988), 104.

26. Ibid., 227 n. 103.

27. Lugones, "On the Logic," 38.

28. Young, *Justice and the Politics of Difference*, 58–61.

29. Ibid., 168–73.

30. Ibid., 171.

31. Ibid.

32. I am influenced in my treatment of power by Wartenberg, *The Forms of Power.*

33. Ibid, 184.

34. A much more elaborate explanation of the process of solidarity is presented in chapter 5.

35. Of course, to bring justice for the poor and oppressed is at the expense of the inordinate material benefits and privileges of the rich and powerful. But justice looked at from this perspective is not at the expense of justice for the rich and powerful but of the injustice that benefits the rich and powerful.

36. John Rawls, *A Theory of Justice* (Cambridge, Mass.: The Belknap Press of Harvard University Press, 1971), 106

37. This refers to Rawls's "difference principle." My use of it does not mean that *mujerista* theology appropriates all aspects of Rawls's analysis and elaboration of justice. However, much of the experience of Latinas bears out several of the key elements of Rawls's conception of justice. This quote

is to be found in Jeffrey Reiman, *Justice and Modern Moral Philosophy* (New Haven: Yale University Press, 1992), 273. Reiman understands justice to be reason's answer to subjugation and sees this theory of justice as providing a much needed foundation for Rawls's difference theory, which he embraces but considers to have a weak foundation based on moral intuition rather than on "moral principles required by reason" (20). For Reiman the difference principle provides the "general structure of social justice" (20). Reiman believes that instead of redistributing goods, what needs to be redistributed are the titles to the labor of others (275).

38. I am grateful to Carmen Torres, one of the Latinas studying in the graduate program at Drew University, for helping me to see the importance of restitution in our account of justice.

39. Here I am not necessarily denying or affirming that we have such right. This is an extremely complex issue that must be dealt with at length. Here I am simply asserting that this is not the main reason for considering restitution as an element of justice.

40. Rawls, *A Theory of Justice*, 102.

41. A more complete delineation of these rights can be found in David Hollenbach, *Justice, Peace and Human Rights* (New York: Crossroad, 1990), 1–125.

42. See María C. Lugones and Elizabeth V. Spelman, "Have We Got a Theory for You! Feminist Theory, Cultural Imperialism and the Demand for 'The Woman's Voice,'" in Marilyn Pearsall, ed., *Women and Values: Readings in Recent Feminist Philosophy* (Belmont, Calif.: Wadsworth Publishing Company, 1986), 26–28.

43. José Porfirio Miranda, *Marx and the Bible: A Critique of the Philosophy of Oppression*, trans. John Eagleson (Maryknoll, N.Y.: Orbis Books, 1974), 61. For a clear and good explanation of the interrelation between love and justice see García, *Justice in Latin American Theology of Liberation*, 99–102.

SEVEN

Elements of a *Mujerista* Anthropology

There are three Spanish phrases that I have come to recognize as critical to the self-understanding of Hispanic women:[1] *la lucha* (the struggle), *permítanme hablar* (allow me to speak), *la comunidad/la familia* (the community/the family). These phrases are repeated with such frequency that they seem to express essential elements of who Latinas are, of how we see ourselves, understand ourselves, value ourselves, construct ourselves, describe ourselves. These phrases that are so common and at the same time so precious for Hispanic women seem to be, therefore, a key to the elaboration of a *mujerista* anthropology. I will explore their meaning in this essay offering them, that is, the phrases and my explorations of their meanings, as elements that need to be considered when elaborating a *mujerista* anthropology, which must have as its source the lived-experience of Latinas and as its goal our liberation.

I am not claiming that these phrases constitute the only elements to be elaborated in a *mujerista* anthropology. Nor am I saying that the understandings they illumine

An earlier version of this chapter was published in Ann O'Hara Graff, ed., *In the Embrace of God: Feminist Approaches to Theological Anthropology* (Maryknoll, N.Y.: Orbis Books, 1995), pp. 90–102.

128

are uniquely ours. But I am saying that they are central and specifically that they come out of our experience as Hispanic women living in the USA. Furthermore, I am saying that these phrases offer a valid starting point for an anthropological exploration of Latinas.

La Lucha

The daily ordinary struggle of Hispanic women to survive and to live fully has been the central element of *mujerista* theology from the very start because it is, I believe, the main experience in the lives of the majority of Latinas. Ever since I learned how hard and difficult life is for grass-roots Hispanic women, I have wondered how they manage to live in the midst of such arduous, demanding, rough and trying reality, in the midst of great suffering. One of my earliest insights, which becomes deeper and clearer with the passing of time, has to do with Hispanic women's ability to deal with suffering without being determined by it. It is an indication that we are unwilling to allow ourselves to be defined by others or by the circumstances over which we have no control. Thus, I have come to see that the insistence on the value of suffering for Christians and its placement as a central element of the Christian message is questionable. I believe, applying a hermeneutics of suspicion, that it has become an ideological tool, a control mechanism used by dominant groups over the poor and the oppressed.

Allow me to make clear what I am saying, using the *via negativa*. I do not negate the reality of suffering in our lives, but I refuse to romanticize it, which I believe is what happens when one ascribes value to suffering in itself. I do not negate the connection between suffering and evil, nor do I dismiss or ignore either of them. I do not negate that

Jesus suffered while he walked in "this valley of tears," but I cannot accept that his suffering was greater than all other human suffering nor that the God whom Jesus called Father demanded or required Jesus to suffer in order to fulfill his mission on earth.

La lucha and not suffering is central to Hispanic women's self-understanding. I have gotten the best clues for understanding how Latinas understand and deal with suffering by looking at Latinas' capacity to celebrate, at our ability to organize a *fiesta* in the midst of the most difficult circumstances and in spite of deep pain. The *fiestas* are, of course, not celebrations of suffering but of the struggle against suffering. The *fiestas* are, very often, a way of encouraging each other not to let the difficulties that are part of Hispanic women's daily life overcome us. They are opportunities to distance ourselves from the rough and arduous reality of everyday life, at times mere escapism, but often a way of getting different perspectives on how to carry on *la lucha*. Listening to the conversations that go on at the *fiestas* and participating in them makes this evident. What one hears is talk about the harshness of life. Of course at times it is a matter of simply complaining. But often it is a matter of sharing with others in order to convince oneself of what one knows: that one is not alone; that what each Hispanic woman is going through is not necessarily, or at least mainly, her fault but is due to oppressive structures. We also hope by talking about it to get the support of others, to get advice and help on how to deal with the situation. *Fiestas* are a very important way for Latinas of not allowing only the suffering in our lives to determine how we perceive life, how we know, how we understand and deal with reality.

An old Latina song says, *la vida buena, es la que se goza,* the good life is the one that one enjoys. This points to the fact that living is, among other things and maybe predominantly, a search for the good life. The struggle for survival, then, is not only a struggle not to die, not only a struggle to live but only barely. It is a struggle to live fully.[2] The struggle for survival is a search for pleasure of those who think of themselves as *familia/comunidad*, "a search for lasting joy, deep delight, gratuitous enjoyment, contagious good fortune."[3] The good life does not ignore suffering. It struggles to go beyond it, to evade it. As a matter of fact, what our *fiestas* suggest is that parties and celebrations are needed in order for Latinas to deal in a creative way with the suffering that surrounds us instead of allowing it to define us. The celebrations that we so easily pull together and enjoy so very much often are opportunities for Hispanic women to "appreciate and accompany the affliction of others with solidarity and tenderness"[4] in *lo cotidiano* — the everyday life — for us.

Lo cotidiano provides a needed framework for explaining *la lucha* as an important element of *mujerista* anthropology. A *mujerista* description of *lo cotidiano* adds to the perspective "from below" the consideration of "from within," and "of our own selves." In other words, *lo cotidiano* for us has to do with the way that we Latinas ourselves consider action, discourse, norms, established social roles, and our own selves. It is precisely when Hispanic women's perspective of reality — including ourselves — is the lens used that *la lucha*, not suffering, is seen as central to Latinas' humanity. Even in the moments of greatest suffering in our lives, if looked at from below and from within, the suffering is not what is most influential in determining how we act, talk, make decisions. Though Hispanic women suffer racial/ethnic and sexist oppression and most of us also suffer poverty, we do not go about our *vida cotidiana* — our everyday life — thinking that we suffer but rather thinking how to struggle to survive, to live fully. We do not

go around saying to ourselves or to others, "I am suffering." Instead we go around saying, "Así es la vida." Many
think that this denotes a certain fatalism. But the *"así es la
vida"* of Latinas goes hand in hand with our *lucha diaria* —
the daily struggle which is the stuff out of which our lives
are made.

It could be argued that *la lucha* and suffering are two
sides of the same coin. But for *mujerista* anthropology there
is a great difference between these two perspectives. Those
who use suffering as their lens and see it as central to Hispanic women's lives historically have idealized suffering in
a way that results in a certain fatalism.[5] I believe Christianity has much to do with this focus. Christianity has tended
to endorse and encourage a certain masochism that has influenced to a great extent the discourse about suffering and
its role in the lives of Latinas. On the other hand from the
inside, from the perspective of Hispanic women, it is the
struggle against oppression and poverty and for liberation
that is central to who we are.[6]

Permítanme Hablar

A *mujerista* anthropology is about Latinas as human beings,
not in the abstract but within the context of our given reality. And it takes into consideration what we understand our
task in history to be. Each and every Hispanic woman as a
"human being is not primarily a definition but rather a history within space and time."[7] Latinas are makers of history.
A *mujerista* anthropology insists on the need to denounce
the way that Hispanic women have been erased from the
histories of our communities and of our countries of origin, and from the history of the USA. This is what the
phrase *permítanme hablar* indicates. We have never been

absent from history but we have been ignored by historical accounts. Therefore, our insistence on speaking, on making known our histories,

> is not a matter of reassuring nostalgia and pleasant reveries. It is a subversive memory, and it lends force and sustenance to our positions, refuses to compromise or equivocate, learns from failures, and knows (by experience) that it has the capability of overcoming every obstacle, even repression itself.[8]

Our insistence on speaking is not only a matter of making known our past; it is also a matter of participating in making present and future history, of being protagonists, of being agents of our own history. If when we speak we are not listened to, if Latinas continue to be spoken to, spoken about, or simply — supposedly — included in what is said about Hispanics in general, our humanity will continue to be diminished not only in the eyes of the dominant group, but also, unfortunately, in our own eyes as we internalize such objectification of ourselves. As long as our voices are not heard, as long as the role we play in history is not recognized and its specificity is not appreciated, we will not be able to become full moral agents, full persons in our own right. This is why we insist that a *mujerista* anthropology has to center on Hispanic women as human beings in time and history; it is an anthropology "from within" and "from below." It recognizes that anthropology is not about an idealized type of humanity or about an abstract understanding of humanity, but that anthropology rises out of a context. Since Latinas are an intrinsic part of that context, our self-understanding cannot be ignored.

There are several difficulties in recognizing and affirming the perspective of Hispanic women about our humanity as a necessary element of all anthropologies. First, when

it comes to women, the well-known split of the private
and the public sphere continues to exist. History is about
the public sphere, and since women are given a role and
some authority — though little power — only in the private sphere, women are mostly absent from written history,
from what is recognized as the official (the "true" version)
of what has happened. Much can be said about this false
dichotomy, but we will limit our comments here to two.
First, what is called history deals mostly with political and
military events. Yet this history does not exist apart from
social history: from history of the family, history of ideas,
history of social and religious movements, history of the
churches and religions. Social history is not mere secondary
history.

Social history deals with that same *lo cotidiano* in which
Latinas are key players. It is important to point out that
lo cotidiano, as defined above, does not have to do only
with what Hispanic women do in our homes, within our
communities, in the activities that one classifies as "Hispanic." *Lo cotidiano* also refers to what Latinas think about
the patterns of action, discourse, norms, and established
social roles of "institutional formations like church, state,
or major economic groups...[that] control real resources,
both symbolic and material, which they use to project messages and power over time, space, and social boundaries."[9]
In other words, Hispanic women are very conscious of how
the world we live in is defined for us, without taking us into
consideration. It is precisely this omission that a *mujerista*
anthropology seeks to denounce and correct.

Another important consideration is this: the history of
social movements is about movements that have been and
are populated and carried out by the common folk, with
women playing a very important role in them.[10] In Hispanic communities religion often plays a key role in many

of these social movements.[11] Though unrecognized by many of the churches' institutions, Latinas are indeed most of the leaders and workers in our communities. Therefore, though receiving very little credit, Hispanic women play an important role within social movements and thus in a true understanding of history. For example, without in any way diminishing the work and leadership provided by César Chávez to the United Farm Workers, it is critical to study, know, and publicly acknowledge the role Dolores Huerta has played and continues to play in the struggle of the UFW as its vice-president. Another example is that of Antonia Pantoja, a Puerto Rican woman who founded ASPIRA, an organization that funds and promotes the education of Puerto Ricans, and who is little known even within Latino communities. These organizations usually have depended more on women than on men to carry out their programs and make effective demands upon the city, state, and industries on behalf of the Latina community.

Besides the desire and capacity of Latinas to have a protagonist role in history, *permítanme hablar* indicates a second difficulty in asserting the role of Latinas' self-understanding and our view of reality as intrinsic to a *mujerista* anthropology. It has to do with the fact that women in general and Hispanic women in particular are considered incapable of reflecting, of thinking, of conceptualizing. As we have always insisted, Hispanic women are not only doers; we are thinkers also. We do engage each other and the society of the USA — our reality — in a critical way. We analyze and we understand. Latinas reflect, and that is a way of making a real contribution to history, to the transformation of history. This is why as *mujeristas* we have always insisted that we must not separate action from reflection. We have always insisted that praxis is reflective action. Because the dominant culture and even our own

Latino brothers often do not recognize Latinas' capacity to think, this is precisely why we have insisted on identifying grassroots Hispanic women as organic intellectuals.[12]

We have been told that to highlight the phrase *permítanme hablar* — allow me to speak — would take power from Latinas, would seem to recognize that others have to give us permission to talk. This common expression might be construed that way if one were to start from the position that Hispanic women have not spoken. But the fact is that we have repeatedly spoken throughout history, that we speak daily, constantly. In highlighting this phrase, I am insisting that people need to pay attention to us, to what we say about ourselves and the reality we and our communities live. When Latinas use the phrase *permítanme hablar,* we are not merely asking to be taken into consideration.[13] When we use this phrase we are asking for a respectful silence from all those who have the power to set up definitions of what it is to be human, a respectful silence so others can indeed hear our cries denouncing oppression and injustice, so others can understand our vision of a just society. We know that if those with power, within as well as outside the Hispanic communities, do not hear us, they will continue to give no credence to the full humanity of Latinas. That is why we insist on the capacity of Hispanic women to speak our own word. For Latinas to speak and to be heard is fundamental in the elaboration of a *mujerista* anthropology for it makes it possible for us to attest to our humanity.

For many Hispanic women who have seldom found anyone to listen to them — to hear them — their *permítanme hablar* is a way of insisting on recognition of our right to think, to defend our rights, to participate in setting what is normative of and for humanity. To demand that we be listened to is a way for us to assert our own identity, to demand that our understanding of our own humanity has to be taken into consideration in the understanding of all humanity. And, given all that we have said, our self-understanding is not divorced from our daily struggle, from our *lucha* to live fully and to bring *lo cotidiano* into the full view of society at large.[14]

La Familia, la Comunidad

Recently several Latinas were sharing our reaction to the often heard comment that Hispanic families are "being destroyed," or "are falling apart." Though some agreed somewhat with these statements, all of us disagreed with this negative view of the status of Latina families. What we all did agree with is that for us *la familia* "is the central and most important institution in life."[15] Whether our family situation is positive or negative, still the ideology of family as central to our lives, to who we are, is primary. This is why it has to be an intrinsic element of a *mujerista* anthropology. But it is important that we understand what kind of *familia* we are talking about. We need to look at how *la familia* has changed, and we must evaluate those changes not by comparing them with the way family has been in our culture, but in view of the role it has today.

It is my contention that the often familiar comment about how poorly the Hispanic family is faring in today's society is a veiled but nonetheless direct accusation of the change in the role of Latinas in our families. I believe, however, that women continue to be the mainstay of our families and that what we are no longer willing to do — in part because more and more of us are gainfully employed outside the home — is to remain married and/or living with men who oppress us and, yes, even mistreat us. Careful observation of Hispanic women who are single mothers is what led me initially to suspect that cries about the demise of Latina families are unfounded. What is really behind such cries is fear of the demise of the patriarchal family, not the destruction of Hispanic families as such.

First of all, we need to question seriously the conclusion which sees Latina families as they move from one generation to another and become acculturated as reaching a point where they stop being ethnic families and become "modern American families."[16] Neither modernization nor acculturation are the major reasons for the changes one can observe in our families, changes that are not anti-Hispanic. Instead it seems that the changes reflect the decreasing need for sex-role differentiation because of technological innovations that make it unnecessary to "reward males with the myth of male superiority."[17] As women acquired more resources and skills, through education and paid employment, "they achieved greater equality in conjugal decision making without sacrificing ethnicity in other realms of family life."[18] The changes have to do mainly with the way we Latinas look upon *machismo* and *hembrismo*. But there is very little credence given, even within our communities, to the reasons for these changes in behavioral attitudes because the dominant culture has successfully projected Latinas and Latinos as primary examples of male chauvinism and female inferiority.

Both *machismo* and *hembrismo* have become concepts that use Spanish nouns as their names. Though indeed both concepts are based on Hispanic ideologies and behaviors, nowadays they are pancultural and refer to "forms of individual deviancy...rarely normative in any culture."[19] What has happened to Latina communities is that the word *machismo* has been adopted in the USA as the accepted term — when speaking in English — to connote

the idea of extreme male chauvinism. Though the word
hembrismo is not used, what it depicts, namely, traditional
feminine roles characterized by weakness, passivity, and
inertia, is considered by the dominant culture to be ex-
emplified by Hispanic women. In other words, Latinas are
the best examples of such female characteristics.[20] Holding Hispanic women and men as exemplars when it comes
to behavioral and ideological deviance is a useful and effi-
cient way for people of the dominant culture, both men and
women, to consider themselves in a superior position to us.

This does not take away from the fact that as Latinas
we have much struggling to do within our families. But in
many ways, family has been Latinas' domain through the
ages. It is in *la familia* that we are agents of our own history, that we can claim a historical role within space and
time, that we make our mark — so to speak — by making
viable future generations and by influencing them. Though
our realm has been a small one compared to the one com-
manded by Hispanic men, it certainly goes way beyond the
small, nuclear family characteristic of the dominant culture.
Our domain, *la familia,* is an amplified family that includes
nuclear family members, particularly the mother and children, plus the extended family — grandparents, cousins two
and three times removed, aunts and uncles, in-laws — plus
comadres and *compadres,* godparents brought into the family
for a variety of reasons. Family for us is a vast network of
relationships and resources in which Hispanic women play
a key role. I believe this is why Latinas want to preserve
our families while ridding ourselves of oppressive elements
and understandings about the family and about our role in
it. Instead of devaluing and rejecting our traditional roles
in our families, what Latinas want is the opposite: we want
the value of those roles to be recognized and their status to
be enhanced.[21] Once this happens we believe Hispanic men

might have an easier time in accepting their responsibilities as sons, brothers, and fathers and will become nurturers and transmitters of family values and ideology. This is of utmost importance if we are to change the terrifying picture of Hispanic children today, with 38.4 percent of them living in poverty.[22]

To understand better the kind of *familia* that is Hispanic women's realm we need to see how in Latina culture the community is an extension, a continuation of the family. As a matter of fact, the importance community has for us follows on the heels of the great significance of family in our culture. To understand the connection between family and community we need to look at *compadrazgo* and *comadrazgo,* the middle point between family and community. *Compadrazgo* and *comadrazgo* extend family and embrace neighbors, and through them Latinas extend our domain to include important members of the community. *Compadrazgo* and *comadrazgo* refer to the system of relationships that are established between godparents and godchildren and between the godparents and the parents of godchildren. *Comadres* and *compadres* — co-mothers and co-fathers — are additional sets of parents who act as guardians or sponsors, caring for the godchildren and providing for them when needed. But the system of *compadrazgo* and *comadrazgo* is extended beyond religious occasions such as baptism and confirmation to secular activities and enterprises. Dances have *madrinas* (godmothers) or *padrinos* (godfathers); so do businesses, sports teams, and religious processions.[23]

The system of *compadrazgo* and *comadrazgo* works because of the significance of "personalism" in our culture. Personalism is "an orientation toward people and persons over concepts and ideas."[24] Therefore, the connections among people are very important. Our amplified families function in many ways because of personal contacts. The more numerous the family, the more widespread the network of "intimate" connections is. So the *compadrazgo* and *comadrazgo* system creates an effective infrastructure of interdependence, with Latinas most of the time being at its center. Through *compadrazgo* and *comadrazgo* family ideology and family values of unity, welfare, and honor reach into the community. It is this amplified family, in many ways a community, that guarantees protection and caretaking for its members as long as we remain faithful to it. It is not hard then to see that, given the importance Hispanic women have within our *familias,* rather than giving up or diminishing the role we have within them, we seek to enhance that role.

One very important area of Hispanic women's self-understanding and self-worth that has not found a positive ambiance in *la familia* is that of embodiment. On the contrary, most of the time it is precisely because of the role we play in our families that we do not have control over our bodies, that our sexuality is restricted and negated, that our bodies are used against ourselves. *Familia/comunidad,* unfortunately, is not a safe place for women when it comes to considerations of Latinas' bodies. The aspects of sexuality that have to do with pleasure, communication, and affection are negated and only procreation is valued. Indeed, the fact that procreation is given such a high value is related to the fact that other aspects of sexuality are denied to us. Our procreative role and the functions connected with it — nurturing and responsibility for the children — most of the time work against us.

Latinas bodies continue to be objectified. Hispanic men as well as other men and women of the dominant culture objectify Hispanic women's bodies. Rape and all forms of irresponsible sex are perhaps the clearest examples of such objectification. Here I am not talking only about the begetting of children but also about the psychological and emotional trauma that sexuality outside of a committed relationship causes many of us. Still another significant form of objectification of Latinas' bodies is exploitation of our physical labor. Many Hispanic women endure sleep deprivation because of the double and triple work burden they bear. Luisa is up by five in the morning and never goes to bed before midnight. She is a single mother with two children. She keeps house, makes a living by working (a bus plus a subway ride away from home) and is trying to finish high school. María is a middle-class woman who has to work outside the home. Her husband helps her with their child and the house. But that is precisely it: he helps; it is her responsibility to bring up their son, to tend to the house even if she works many more hours than he does and earns more than double the amount of money he does.

Exploitation of the labor of Latinas is clear in the lack of available household conveniences that could ease the physical work we have to do to survive. And here I remember my own grandmother, who suffered from a very young age of a heart condition brought on by arthritis, caused in part by her exhausting work as a washerwoman. But then, as a single mother of two girls and without much schooling, what else could she do to survive? Disregard for our bodies continues the custom among Hispanics for women to be served food last, for Latinas to consider it their obligation to give their food to the children and men and if necessary to go hungry themselves. I have seen this happen many times including yesterday, when I went to visit a friend in *el barrio,* East Harlem. And this is not something that happens only among poor Latinas. For example, in my middle-class family, my mother insists on serving my father, brothers, and brothers-in-law better and bigger portions of food. All of this, I believe is grounded in the objectification of Latinas' bodies, in the exploitation of our bodies.

Again, what is most worrisome about this is that Hispanic women have internalized — and continue to internalize — such negativity about our bodies. The negation of sexuality as a key element of our humanity, lack of understanding that our bodies are ourselves, is one of the main reasons, I believe, for the self-loathing of our teenagers, for the irresponsible way in which they "use" their bodies. We lack an understanding of the intrinsic-ness of our bodies to who we are, of the fact that we are at all times embodied beings, and that every human being is one single entity of body-spirit. Unfortunately, *familia/comunidad* is a negative factor in this area because it insists on and supports oppressive sexual relationships, with both Hispanic men as well as Hispanic women being victims.

Yet *familia/comunidad* is women's domain because it is a distinct arena where we are historical protagonists. It is also what provides Latinas repeatedly with a sense of unity and cohesiveness, with a sense of self-identity and self-worth. *Familia/comunidad* relies on interdependence and this allows some space for Hispanic women to be counted, to be considered important, and, therefore, to be dealt with in a respectful way, to be valued as a person and not just because of what we do. *Familia/comunidad* for Latinas/os does not subsume the person but rather emphasizes that the person is constituted by this entity and that the individual person and the community have a dialogic relationship through which the person reflects the *familia/comunidad* "out of which it was born, yet, as in a prism, that reflection is also a refraction. . . . In an authentic [family]/community, the identity of the 'we' does not extinguish the 'I'; the Spanish word for 'we' is *'nosotros,'* which literally means 'we others,' a community of *otros,* or others."[25] In *familia/ comunidad* the "I" of Hispanic women is heard and embraced without fear for it does not in any way threaten the "we."

This is not in any way an attempt to romanticize Latina families and communities or to downplay conflicts and the oppression we suffer even within what I claim to be "our domain." There is strife in our families and communities, and unity of interests often does not exist there. But the fact is that *familia/comunidad* is a cultural value. Often it is the first and last recourse for survival for Hispanics. *Familia/comunidad* is a grounding element for Latinas, for our self-understanding, and, therefore, must be a central element in a *mujerista* anthropology.

Conclusion

Since the goal of all *mujerista* enterprise is the liberation of Latinas, a *mujerista* anthropology seeks to illumine how we understand ourselves, how we perceive and construct ourselves as human beings with a history and within a time frame of existence, how we live our women-selves, which is the only way we can live our human-selves. No narrative, no discourse can capture the richness of our own experience, of our searching for opportunities to be fully who we are, of our amazement when we discover how roles have defined us and limited us while at the same time realizing the potential richness of such roles.

A *mujerista* anthropology is definitely framed by *la lucha,* not a struggle against anyone or anything but for recognition of the fullness of our humanity as women-selves, and on behalf of all persons.[26] To do this we have to repeat constantly, *permítame hablar,* because as Latinas we are about begetting new realities for ourselves and for our *familias/comunidades*. We are about giving birth to a new understanding of humanity that starts by insisting on a protagonist role for all persons, and a society based on understandings of interdependence, while embracing differences that are at the heart of what it means for us to be *familia*.

Notes

1. There is no agreement among Latinas/Hispanics as to what to call ourselves. In this article I will take turns using both terms.

2. Ada María Isasi-Díaz and Yolanda Tarango, *Hispanic Women: Prophetic Voice in the Church* (San Francisco: Harper and Row, 1988; reprint Minneapolis: Fortress Press, 1992), 4. See also Otto Maduro, *Mapas para la fiesta* (Buenos Aires: Centro Nueva Tierra para la Promoción Social y Pastoral, 1992), 25–27.

3. Maduro, *Mapas para la fiesta*, 25–27.

4. Ibid.

5. It is undoubtedly true that as Latinas we have a *sentido trágico de la vida* — a tragic sense of life. But this tragic sense is much more tied to the emotionalism and hyperbolic sense of Latina character than to fatalism. This is particularly true of the strands of Latina culture that have a strong African influence. The strands of Latina culture that have more of an Amerindian influence might be considered to be somewhat fatalistic. But one has to understand the role that the magical or supernatural or surreal or psychic plays in Amerindian cultures — and by extension in Latina culture — before one talks about our fatalism.

6. See M. Shawn Copeland, "'Wading through Many Sorrows': Toward a Theology of Suffering in Womanist Perspective," in Emilie M. Townes, ed., *A Troubling in My Soul* (Maryknoll, N.Y.: Orbis Books, 1993), 109–29. To me it is significant that though Copeland sets out to elaborate "a theology of suffering," she finishes by pointing out that the focus for African American women is not suffering but resistance.

7. Ivone Gebara and Maria Clara Bingemer, *Mary: Mother of God, Mother of the Poor* (Maryknoll, N.Y.: Orbis Books, 1989), 11.

8. Gustavo Gutiérrez, *The Power of the Poor in History* (Maryknoll, N.Y.: Orbis Books, 1983), 80.

9. Daniel H. Levine, *Popular Voices in Latin American Catholicism* (Princeton, N.J.: Princeton University Press, 1992), 317.

10. It is always important to remember that women are more than half the world population. With very few exceptions, like Alaska and Australia, we are more than half of the population of all countries.

11. Gutiérrez insists that often the spiritual movements of the poor are social movements as well. See Gutiérrez, *The Power of the Poor,* 94.

12. Isasi-Díaz and Tarango, *Hispanic Women,* 7–9.

13. Nelly Ritchie, "SER MUJER — Parte integral de una eclesiología en marcha," in María Pilar Aquino, ed., *Aportes para una teología desde la mujer* (Madrid: Biblia y Fe, 1988), 107.

14. Cf. Carmen Lora Ames, "Implicaciones teológicas en la experiencia de las organizaciones femeninas en el ámbito de la vida cotidiana," paper presented at the Maryknoll School of Theology, January 1987 (photocopied); quoted in María Pilar Aquino, *Our Cry for Life* (Maryknoll, N.Y.: Orbis Books, 1993), 92.

15. Roberto R. Alvarez, Jr., "The Family," in Nicolás Kanellss, ed., *The Hispanic American Almanac* (Washington, D.C.: Gale Research, 1993), 155.

16. Oscar Ramírez and Carlos H. Arce, "The Contemporary Chicano Family: An Empirically Based Review," in Augustine Barón, Jr., ed., *Explorations in Chicano Psychology* (New York: Praeger Publishers, 1981), 19.

17. Melba J. T. Vásquez and Anna M. González, "Sex Roles among Chicanos: Stereotypes, Challenges, and Changes," in Barón, *Explorations,* 63.

18. Ibid.

19. Ramírez and Arce, "The Contemporary Chicano Family," 63.

20. The term *hembrismo* was coined in 1955 by M. E. Bermúdez in her book on Mexican family life. Since *macho* means male and *hembra* means female, Bermúdez created the term *hembrismo* to parallel *machismo.* See Vásquez and González, "Sex Roles among Chicanos," 51–52.

21. Ibid.

22. The breakdown of Hispanic children living in poverty is as follows: Mexican American: 36.3 percent; Cuban: 31.0 percent; Puerto Rican: 56.7 percent; Central and South American: 35.2 percent. These figures were reported in *Hispanic Magazine,* August 1993, 12. They are taken from the USA Bureau of the Census.

23. In English one would talk about the sponsor of a dance or of a business rather than of a godfather or godmother. There is a Spanish word for sponsor — *patrocinador/a* — which is also used when the special sense of *compadrazgo* is not intended.

24. Guillermo Bernal, "Cuban Families," in Monica McGoldrick,

John K. Pearce, and Joseph Giordano, eds., *Ethnicity and Family Therapy* (New York: The Guilford Press, 1982), 192.

25. "*Nosotros:* Toward a U.S. Hispanic Anthropology," *Listening — Journal of Religion and Culture* 27, no. 1 (Winter 1992): 57.

26. Ritchie, "SER MUJER — Parte integral de una eclesiología en marcha," 105–7.

La Palabra de Dios en Nosotras
The Word of God in Us

I never read the Bible. Once in school I had a Bible class, and it was just like any other subject, like you read a history book. I only know the passages that are read at Mass on Sundays. And I do not have the least idea of what is the Old Testament. Bible to me is an unknown subject....I remember my Bible, they made us buy it one year, and we read it a couple of times....All that about reading the Bible is very American. In Cuba the Bible was not important.[1]

Though there are Hispanic women whose relationship to the Bible is different from this Latina's, she is representative of how the majority of Hispanic women relate to the Bible. The actual way in which Hispanic women regard the Bible, no matter how peripheral it is, provides the starting point for an articulation of a *mujerista* biblical interpretation.

An earlier version of this chapter was published in Elisabeth Schüssler Fiorenza, ed., *Searching the Scriptures*, vol. 1: *A Feminist Introduction* (New York: Crossroad, 1993), pp. 86–97. Copyright © 1993 by The Crossroad Publishing Company. Adapted with permission of The Crossroad Publishing Co., New York; SCM Press, Ltd., London; and HarperCollins*Religious*, Melbourne.

Main Elements of
Mujerista Biblical Interpretation

Elsewhere we have begun to articulate the main elements of a critical *mujerista* interpretation of the Bible.[2] We present them here briefly. First, there exists a Hispanic Christianity, a *mestiza* and *mulata* Christianity, heavily influenced by the Catholicism of the *conquistadores,* a religious practice with little biblical content.[3] To this were added religious understandings and practices of African and Amerindian religions. As Protestant and evangelical traditions have become part of the religious understandings and practices of an increasing number of Latinas, we need to find a way to appropriate the central elements of these traditions as they are understood and practiced by Hispanic women so they can become part of our *mestiza* and *mulata* Christianity. The centrality of the Bible in these faith traditions, the influence they have in the dominant culture, and the number of Latinas who are becoming members of Protestant and evangelical churches indicate the urgency there is to articulate a *mujerista* biblical interpretation.[4]

Second, Hispanic women's experience and our struggle for survival, not the Bible, are the source of our theology and the starting point for how we should interpret, appropriate, and use the Bible.[5] A great number of Latinas do not consult the Bible in our daily lives. The complexity of the biblical writings, the variety of messages, and the differences in sociohistorical and political-economic context make it difficult for us to use the Bible. When we need help we find it not in the Bible but in praying to God and the saints: God, Mary, the saints — all part of the divine — to whom Hispanic women have the direct access they do not have to the Bible, which needs interpretation.[6]

Third, the critical lens of *mujerista* theology is liberation. For us liberation starts with survival, both physical
and cultural. As *mujerista* theology struggles to discern how
to appropriate and use the Bible, we must apply to it the
same liberative lens that we use in all our theological work.
Therefore, from the start we can say that a *mujerista* biblical hermeneutic submits the Bible to a Latinas' liberative
canon. This means that the Bible is to be accepted as part
of divine revelation and becomes authoritative for us only
insofar as it contributes to our struggle for liberation.[7]

Two caveats are in order here. For the great majority
of Hispanic women, the marginal way they deal with the
Bible is not a conscious decision. We do not reject the
Bible; we simply do not use it or use it very sparingly and
selectively. Second, since Latinas' lived experience is the
source of *mujerista* theology, the task of *mujerista* theologians is to articulate the religious practice of Hispanic
women. We do this to help our communities become aware
of how their religious beliefs operate in our daily lives. Our
task is to analyze those practices through a liberative lens
and to evaluate them in view of the liberation of Latinas. Because *mujerista* theologians are an integral part of
the Latina community, part of our task is to participate
with the community in deciding how Hispanic women will
relate to and use the Bible from now on.[8]

There are three important elements in *mujerista* biblical interpretation. First, the mostly unarticulated criterion
that has guided the Latinas' usage of the Bible has been
need. We have used it when we have needed it, for what
we have needed it, in the manner we have needed. Second,
the struggle for liberation has to be the critical lens of our
biblical hermeneutics. Third, Hispanic women's interpretation of the Bible is central to identifying and struggling
for our *proyecto histórico,* our preferred future, which we be-

lieve is an intrinsic part of the unfolding of the kin-dom of God.[9]

Need: Latinas' Guide to the Bible

How have and how do grassroots Hispanic women approach and use the Bible? The majority of Latinas know the Bible mostly from hearing it read on Sundays in their churches; they know the Bible through oral tradition rather than through reading and studying the biblical text.[10] They listen and tell biblical stories; they refer to the Bible in their discussions and struggles not because they believe — or do not believe — that it is the word of God, and that as such it tells them what to do or not to do. Latinas use Bible stories hoping to find someone in the story who will be a source of hope: "others have survived similar circumstances, so will I." Hispanic women have traditionally listened to and told Bible stories as a source of strength, in order to understand what is happening to us.

Recently at a national conference of Latinas, the speaker was trying to find a way of explaining how Hispanic women need to stand up, to insist on our rights as much as possible without endangering ourselves and our family. She decided to use a Bible story and in doing so mixed elements of two different biblical pericopes.

> The woman in the Bible who needed help? Well, she realized Jesus could help her and nothing was going to stop her. It was not very nice, as a matter of fact, it was terrible of Jesus to tell her that she could not eat from the bread that was on the table. She could only have crumbs. If it had been me, I would have answered him that he should not talk that way to

me, that I have every right to eat from the bread on the table. We do not want just the crumbs, no. (Applause) Well, she insisted on her right; she took it without Jesus giving it to her. Jesus knew that power had gone out of him; that she had taken power in her own hands because she and her daughter were in great need.[11]

No one seemed to have noticed that the speaker had confused two stories, or, if they noticed, it did not matter, for what gave authority to that text was not the way it was written in the Bible but the way it had been appropriated by this Latina and the way it could be of help to the rest of us.

Those in the Bible who struggled for survival, including Jesus, are one of the few "reality checks" that Latinas have. Society questions our reality and makes us question it by objectivizing us, instrumentalizing us. Society alienates us unless we are willing to participate in it on the terms of the dominant culture.[12] Anyone, including biblical persons, who has gone through situations similar to ours encourages us to believe in ourselves and our communities. All such persons and examples help us know that we are not imagining things, that though we are often rendered invisible by those who have power, we do not cease to exist.

The sense that the people of *our* Bible stories, stories that come from a book we know is important, can understand us because they have also had to struggle for survival is important to Hispanic women. Bible stories become *ours* when we use them because we need to, and to make them be helpful in a given situation we change even central elements of the story itself, highlighting perhaps nonessential elements.[13] It is not that the integrity of the text is not important; it is that the need to survive takes precedence.

Being linked to the people of *our* Bible stories extends our community to include those of ages past. We know our struggle is an ancient one; *our* Bible stories put us in touch with other ancient histories of struggle; they help us realize that as a community of struggle we have existed for many, many centuries. *Our* biblical stories put us in contact with the communities of our forebears and teach us that though we must struggle with all our might against oppression; we must not grow weary.[14] By making us part of a much wider community of struggle, biblical stories help us hold on to the belief that *se hace lo que se puede,* one does what is possible. It helps us continue to understand that though we may not be able to solve problems, to remedy the terrible situation in which we live, we can make a positive contribution. Partial solutions are elements of the transformative change because the struggle to bring them about provides inspiration and can indeed provide the favorable conditions others need to be able to struggle for liberation.[15]

We must pass on to our children the sense of struggle that permeates our lives so that they too will have a heritage of resistance and courageous action. We have "neither gold nor silver," but we have *our* biblical stories, as well as the many stories of struggle and survival that circulate in our communities to pass on to our children.

Living into Our Preferred Future: *Nuestro Proyecto Histórico*

An element of liberation-salvation that needs elaboration because it impinges on *mujerista* biblical hermeneutics is our preferred future, our *proyecto histórico.* Before discussing our *proyecto histórico,* two preliminary points need to be made. First, our insistence on liberation carries with it a rejection of equality within the present socio-political-economic structures. We believe these structures are based on an oppressive understanding of power: power as domination and control. These structures necessitate a group in need, unemployed, considered as a diminished sector of humanity, that can be used to maintain the privileges of the few. If Hispanics "move ahead" in society, necessarily another group of people will have to take our place as "the diminished sector of society" within the system. Our goal, therefore, is not to partake of the privileges of those who now control and dominate us. Instead we seek to change radically present oppressive structures so nobody will be diminished.

Second, an in-depth analysis of the way oppressive structures work makes it evident that oppressed groups are set one against the other for the benefit of those with power. As we struggle to make our *proyecto histórico* a reality we are committed to do all we can not to be involved in horizontal violence: not to act against other oppressed groups in this society and worldwide. Our liberation as Latinas cannot be at the expense of anyone. Though our strategies may be different from those of other racial/ethnic groups, we cannot have goals and strategies that contradict or act against the legitimate struggles of other oppressed groups for liberation. But neither will we allow ourselves to be used, as we have done in the past. We will not postpone our struggle for liberation any longer.

Our *proyecto histórico* relates to and shapes our articulation of *mujerista* biblical hermeneutics in four concrete ways. First, theology, including biblical exegesis, is for us a praxis. The study and interpretation of Scripture by Hispanic women is a revolutionary act for neither our churches nor the academy consider us capable of doing it, consider that we have something to contribute in this field. Therefore, doing biblical exegesis is a way of claiming our right to think, to know critically — it is an element in our self-definition. We must also insist on theology, biblical exegesis included, as a communal task. The values and needs of the community must play a central role in *mujerista* biblical hermeneutics, and the only way to make sure this is so is by doing theology as a community of faith and struggle.[16]

The second way is best illustrated by the example of three women. Talking to María a few years ago, I found out that she attends a Protestant church. But she also had her daughter baptized in the Catholic Church, because, "I'm still a Catholic." Margarita is a Catholic who goes to Mass weekly. "But I also go to other churches with my friends," she adds. Doña Inés was a stalwart member of a Lutheran church. The Lutheran pastor visited her in the hospital where she was dying. Doña Inés managed to ask the pastor to pray with her. In an almost inaudible, raspy voice she started praying, *"Dios te salve, María,"* a common prayer to Mary used in the Roman Catholic tradition, the faith tradition of Doña Inés's youth.

These and other Latinas are most comfortable recognizing diverse manifestations of the divine as well as diverse expressions of the relationship between human beings and the divine. Their functional religious pluralism, "grassroots ecumenism," moves beyond traditional doctrinal purity and emerges as religious solidarity, which becomes a source of motivation, strength, and strategies in our daily struggles.[17] The amplification and extension of this experience of ecumenism among Hispanic women is an intentional element of our *proyecto histórico*. For this to happen, we all have to overcome the prejudices we have against Hispanics of different faith traditions, we have to stop discriminating against one another because of race, nation of origin, and economic status.

A third element of our *proyecto histórico* linked to the previous one that has to be taken into consideration and enhanced by *mujerista* interpretation, appropriation, and use of the Bible is that of reconstituting church structures. If we are to live into our preferred future we have to demand that our churches give concrete and obvious witness not only by what they say but also by the kind of institutions they are. Most of the institutional structures of our churches respond mostly to the exigencies of the status quo instead of effectively serving the community of faith. Specifically there are two elements which we insist must change. One is the hierarchical self-understanding that permeates our churches and expresses itself not only in the way the ministers of the churches are organized but also in how they relate to the laity, in the churches' understanding of truth, relationship, and "fullness of being." The other element that has to be changed is the privileges that society accords to most of the churches and what the churches do with those privileges. Churches must first admit that they do have these privileges and that those in positions of power in the churches enjoy them and benefit from them. Then those individuals who benefit from these privileges should be accountable to the community as to how they use them.[18] Hierarchical understandings and structures as well as ecclesiastical privileges are at the heart of elitism, one of the greatest temptations that churches have yielded to historically. Latinas have suffered too much and too long because of elitism not to demand its elimination from our preferred future.

A fourth element to consider as we struggle to live into our preferred future has to do with the socio-political-economic reality in which we live. The particularities of this reality are beyond the scope of this article but we need at least to enumerate the main ones. First, we reject a split between the personal and the political because moral agency requires us to take responsibility for social as well as for interpersonal life. Second, social theories used to explain and construct society must respect the self-determination of the person — person being always understood as a human being in relation with a community. Third, an analysis and redefinition of power are essential if we are to participate in the development of a just society. Fourth, moral criteria for evaluation of public policy have to include in a prominent way the understanding of liberation and the right of all groups to struggle to achieve liberation. Fifth, achieving the common good must be the central goal of societal structures, institutions and policies. By common good we understand at the very least a society in which all have access to what they need to achieve dignity and meaning in life as members of a community to which they are accountable. To assure this we need, among other things, a national commitment to full employment and an adequate minimum wage; redistribution of wealth through redistributive inheritance and wealth taxes; comparable remuneration for comparable work regardless of sex, sexual preference, race/ethnicity, age, etc.; economic democracy that would transform an economy controlled by a few to the economy of a participatory community; health care — particular emphasis being needed on preventive health care — available to all; changes in the economics of the family that will encourage more "symmetrical marriages, allow a better balance between family and work for both men and women, and make parenting a less difficult and impoverishing act for single parents," the majority of whom are women;[19] access to political office of Hispanic women and men so as to insure adequate representation of our community; restructuring of the educational system so that our children and all those interested can study Hispanic culture and Spanish; restructuring the financing of public education so that its quality does not depend on the economics of those who live in the neighborhood served by a given school but is the responsibility of the whole community of that area, region, or state.

Our *proyecto histórico* is part of what situates Latinas. It is our vision of the future and, as such, it is an intrinsic element of our worldview that influences how we see ourselves. Our *proyecto histórico* is both, one of the reasons why we struggle for liberation daily, and it is a central part of our goal.

Appropriating the Bible and Liberative Praxis

For Hispanic women the *palabra de Dios* is not necessarily what is written in the Bible, but refers to the unflinching belief that God is with us in our daily struggles.[20] Years ago in Lima, Perú, where I was living at the time, I used to go to a church in one of the poor *barriadas* that surround the capital. At the back of the church there was a huge banner that read: *"La palabra de Dios tiene fuerzas y da vida."* These words, taken from Hebrews 4:12, had become very meaningful in the life of the community. For them *la palabra de Dios* referred not to what is written in the Bible, but to their understanding that their religious beliefs and practices could help them in their struggle for survival, and that the church, represented for them by the parish priest, was willing to participate with them in that struggle.

This community in Lima understood *la palabra de Dios* similarly to the way Latinas in the USA do today. Such understanding must be the critical lens through which *mujerista* theologians look at the Bible. How do we interpret

and appropriate the Bible so that it becomes an effective
tool in the struggle for liberation? We start by asserting
that in order to survive, to be liberated, we have to develop and strengthen our moral agency as Hispanic women.
Liberation for Hispanic women, as well as for all oppressed people, revolves around the process of becoming
agents of our own history, *sujetos de nuestra historia,* and
this cannot be achieved unless one becomes a strong moral
agent capable of making choices, of acting, of challenging,
and of creating meaning for ourselves in the midst of the
oppressive structures in which we live.[21]

The interpretation, appropriation and use of the Bible,
therefore, for Hispanic women has to enable and enhance
Latinas' moral agency. This is why we are concerned about
the growth of the role of the Bible in the life of Latinas. First, at present those Hispanic women who use the
Bible have little or nothing to say most of the time about
the way the Bible is interpreted. This results in accepting as authoritative an interpretation of the Bible and an
understanding of its importance and usage that is outside
ourselves, not of our own making, not controlled by us,
and, therefore, something that could be used to control us.
Second, a nonbiblical Christianity has been a good vehicle for the inclusion of Amerindian and African beliefs
and practices in our *mestiza* and *mulata* Christianity, an
inclusion that is at the heart of popular religiosity. It is
questionable whether this process of *mestizaje* and *mulatez*
will be able to continue if Latinas do not have a say on how
to interpret, apply, and use the Bible.[22]

From the perspective of moral agency, popular religiosity enables Hispanic women to claim a Christianity that
they, and not the church authorities (largely made up of
non-Hispanic males) determine. Most Latinas who use the
Bible at present do so under the tutelage of priests and pas-

tors, who interpret it and control its interpretation and use in the Hispanic churches. If we do not have a say, the Bible will be imposed on us as the only or the definitive revelation of God to the exclusion of the ongoing revelation of God in our lives and in non-Christian religions.

The third concern we have regarding appropriation of the Bible is how to deal with it when it already plays a role in the life of a growing number of Hispanic women — mainly those who are evangelical or charismatic, whether from a Roman Catholic or Protestant perspective, and those who are Pentecostals.[23] These Latinas use the Bible almost exclusively in an individualistic and pietistic way. Though we consider this usage of the Bible questionable insofar as development and enhancement of moral agency is concerned, it could be an acceptable starting place. But Hispanic women must insist on rejecting a fundamentalist interpretation of the Bible because of the patriarchal worldview that undergirds it and the specific oppressive understandings about women that one finds throughout it. Therefore, given the reality of the oppression of Hispanic women, our appropriation and usage cannot be only pietistic and individualistic, concerned only with a private sense of salvation and used mainly for the consolation of the individual. Such usage has to be denounced whenever it oppresses Hispanic women or supports and promotes understandings and structures that oppress us. As *mujeristas* we are concerned with the way the Bible is interpreted and used to reject or ignore an understanding of structural sin, the social implications of personal salvation, and the intrinsic relationship between struggle for survival and salvation — between struggling for justice in this world and salvation and life everlasting. The Bible should help us to understand the oppression we suffer because of injustices in our world; the Bible should call us as a community of faith to struggle for justice so as to participate in the unfolding of the kin-dom of God.[24]

For *mujerista* theology the enablement and enhancement of moral agency go hand in hand with a process of conscientization, an ongoing process of critical reflection on action that leads to a critical awareness of oppressive structures and their interconnectedness.[25] In this critical process the Bible should be used to learn how to learn — to involve the people in an "unending process of acquiring new pieces of information that multiply the previous store of information."[26] The Bible is a rich resource of "new information": stories of valiant women, of struggles against unbelievable odds, of communities of resistance, of women who found ways to survive in the midst of the worst oppression. This "new information" helps to make obvious problems that may have existed for a long time but ones we have failed to recognize. This usage of the Bible does not apply what the Bible says directly to our situations. The Bible is seen as influencing the formation of the moral character of Latinas. The Bible could play an important role as Hispanic women reflect on who we are as Christians and what our attitudes, dispositions, goals, values, norms, and decisions should be if we are always keeping in mind that our goal is our liberation and the liberation of our people.[27]

A Bible Story as Interpretive Key[28]

One way to use the Bible in keeping with our *mujerista* biblical hermeneutics is to use Bible stories as interpretive keys in our struggle for liberation. In looking at specific biblical passages as interpretive keys, we use them to help us understand the questions we need to ask, questions that shed light on the oppressive situations we *mujeristas* face today. Interpretive keys do not demand compliance to a given archetype or prototype, but rather help us to be critical about the situation at hand. An interpretive key helps us ask questions instead of insisting that it can provide answers. When we use the Bible this way, we claim that the starting point is always the situation at hand and not the Bible. As an interpretive key, no biblical passage can be the deciding factor in our lives. Seeing certain passages of the Bible as an interpretive key allows *mujeristas* to be self-determining — to be the ones that decide what to do and how to do it.[29]

An example of a biblical story *mujeristas* use as an interpretive key is that of Shiphrah and Puah. These two women stand at the beginning of the most formidable and formative event for the Hebrew people, the exodus event. Their story in Exodus 1:15–22 helps raise questions about what should be our role as *mujeristas* in the struggle for our own liberation and the liberation of our people.

Exodus 1:15–22[30] starts with an order from the pharaoh: Shiphrah and Puah[31] are to kill sons born to Hebrew women. Though a man, the pharaoh, stands at the beginning of the narrative, it is not his action but rather the actions of these women that are of primary concern.[32] The pharaoh attempts to deal with the growing number of Hebrews.[33] However, had he been able to foresee the persistence of the women in thwarting his decree, he might have been more successful in his attempt to check the Hebrew population growth by ordering all female infants to be killed![34]

Were these two midwives Egyptian or Hebrew? The Massoretic text reads "Hebrew midwives."[35] But a minor variation in the grammatical forms yields "midwives of the Hebrews," which is the way the Septuagint and the Vulgate read.[36] The ambiguity of the text introduced by the

variation can be seen as a way of moving "beyond na-
tionalistic concerns to bear witness to the power of faith
to transcend ethnic boundaries."[37] Uncertainty, then, about
the midwives' nationality allows us to suggest that the main
moving force and motivating principle of their action was
the fear of God.

Fear in this text is not fear of punishment. The fear
of God that Shiphrah and Puah felt was generated by a
sense of *mysterium tremendum,* "a mystery in divine holiness which produces ... a sense of terror."[38] This sense of
terror is not merely negative but is also an expression of
faith, trust, love, and communion, based on God's unmer-
ited, gratuitous, unearned love. The defiant act of Shiphrah
and Puah makes life for the Hebrews possible, and their
risky, clever answer to the pharaoh, which puts them in
immediate danger, is born out of their own relationship
with God. Their fear of God "becomes the principle of
human behavior and the beginning of wisdom,"[39] making
them mother, life-givers of the Hebrew people.

A literary analysis of this pericope further strengthens
the image of the midwives as life-givers. The pericope por-
trays the pharaoh as the source of death. In contrast the
midwives are portrayed as the source of life. Between the
role of the pharaoh and that of Shiphrah and Puah "stands
the fear of God as a motivating factor (v. 17) and as an
attitude of faith which reaps its reward (v. 21a)."[40] They
are blessed with a progeny: "So God dealt well with the
midwives; and the people multiplied and grew very strong.
And because the midwives feared God he gave them families." This reward, though there is no clear way of reading
verses 20–21, is a reward that corresponds to Shiphrah's
and Puah's deed.[41] Furthermore, this reward seems to indicate that Shiphrah and Puah "are credited with building up
the house of Israel."[42]

The story of Shiphrah and Puah foreshadows the exodus event. Their defiant attitude toward the pharaoh foreshadows the attitude of Moses and Aaron. Like the pharaoh with whom Moses and Aaron will have to deal, this pharaoh becomes increasingly stubborn. The midwives' brave stance forces the pharaoh to escalate his strategy. His attempt to finish with the Hebrews will "force God's hand." Remembering the covenant made with the Israelites, God will intervene in their behalf. The exodus movement has started. Secondly, Shiphrah and Puah save the Israelites. Their actions make the exodus possible. No liberation is possible without courage to act and willingness to risk; these women are indeed risk-takers, agents of their own history and the history of their people.

As an interpretive key that can be used by *mujeristas*, the story of Shiphrah and Puah raises many questions that we apply to our situation today. Often caught against our will between the oppressor and the oppressed, how can we, Hispanic women, be self-determining? How can we be about liberation, no matter what our role in life is? When we do not have power or strategic advantage, do we give in or do we find a way to resist? Can we sacrifice one for the sake of the many? Can a few be liberated at the expense of others? What is the critical lens that *mujeristas* must use all the time: Hispanic-ness or liberation? How does the God of *mujeristas* differ from the God of the pharaohs of our days, of the God who the pharaohs of our world believe themselves to be? How do we as oppressed persons remain faithful to our God?

Each *mujerista* must allow Shiphrah and Puah to ask her many different questions. These questions will produce not jarring pieces but rather elements that will come together to form a tapestry of the whole. Such a weaving will depict a vision of justice that is intrinsic to *mujeristas'* task: our liberation and the liberation of our people.[43]

Notes

1. Words of a Cuban woman living in Miami who considers her way of life "the most Christian she can be." Cited in Ada María Isasi-Díaz and Yolanda Tarango, *Hispanic Women: Prophetic Voice in the Church* (San Francisco: Harper and Row, 1988; reprint Minneapolis: Fortress Press, 1992), 27–28.

2. See my article "The Bible and *Mujerista* Theology, in Susan Brooks Thistlethwaite and Mary Potter Engel, eds., *Lift Every Voice: Constructing Christian Theologies from the Underside* (San Francisco: Harper and Row, 1990), 261–69. Also Isasi-Díaz and Tarango, *Hispanic Women*.

3. Because of the centrality of *mestizaje* and *mulatez* to our self-understanding, we use "*mestiza* and *mulata* Christianity" to refer to Christianity as practiced by Hispanic women.

4. In 1986 the Religion Gallup Poll found that 19 percent of Hispanics identified themselves as Protestants. Using data gathered by the University of Chicago's National Opinion Research Center, sociologist Andrew Greeley concluded in 1988 that about 23 percent of all Hispanics were Protestants and that approximately 60,000 Hispanics join Protestant denominations every year. See Roberto Suro, "Switch by Hispanic Catholics Changes Face of U.S. Religion," *New York Times*, May 14, 1989.

5. It is my experience that even those Latinas who claim the Bible as the starting point of their theology in reality mean *their* reading of the Bible, obviously influenced by their experiences as the basis of their theological enterprise.

6. As a *mujerista* theologian I am an insider/outsider: an insider because I am a Hispanic woman; an outsider because of my formal education and economic status. This sense of insider/outsider is reflected in what could be considered an inconsistent use of "I/we/they/us/my/our/their" throughout this essay.

7. Given that for the majority of Latinas this is a "first" moment in using the Bible, stressing that we accept as authoritative only biblical texts that are liberative to us is a must. This will be an effective guide for Hispanic women. We do recognize that it will be a long time before our refusal to accept oppressive parts of the Bible as "the word of God" is heard by those who use it to control us. But using the Bible to enhance the moral agency of Latinas will certainly weaken its power as an oppressive tool.

8. A few years ago a young, middle-class Latina who had not been intimately connected to the Hispanic community came for the first time to a conference of LAS HERMANAS — a national organization of Hispanic women of faith who struggle in church and society for justice for ourselves and our people. The young Latina knew me from working with me in groups that are mostly Anglo and thought of me as an outsider to the community gathered there. When she complained about my active participation in the conference to one of the organizers, she was told, "Ada is a full member of this organization and of this community; her work as a theologian does not separate her from the rest of us and much less does it place her above us. This is home for her and she does not have to be careful about what she says or how much she says."

9. We use "kin-dom" instead of "kingdom" because the latter is obviously a sexist word that presumes that God is male; second, the concept of kingdom is both hierarchical and elitist — that is why we do not use "reign." "Kin-dom" makes it clear that when the fullness of God becomes a reality, we will all be sisters and brothers — kin to each other.

10. This element of orality is also present in the African American community. See Vincent Wimbush, "The Biblical Historical Study as Liberation: Toward an Afro-Christian Hermeneutics," in Gayraud Wilmore, ed., *African American Religious Studies: An Interdisciplinary Anthology* (Durham, N.C.: Duke University Press, 1989), 140–54. For an explanation of the fact that illiteracy is not necessarily the main reason for Hispanic women not reading the Bible see my article in *Lift Every Voice*, esp. 263–65. See also Isasi-Díaz and Tarango, *Hispanic Women*, 67–70.

11. Since whenever I relate events like this one non-Hispanics always seem to take for granted that I am talking about a Latina who has little formal education, let me say that the speaker is a professor and has a Ph.D. in literature from a reputable USA university. When I talked to her about mixing the stories she said, "I certainly have much to learn about the Bible." I replied, "And I have much to learn about the excellent way in which you appropriated it and used it to enable and encourage the women at this conference."

12. For an important explanation of this point see María Lugones, "Playfulness, 'World'-Travelling, and Loving Perception," *Hypatia* 2, no. 2 (Summer 1987): 3–19.

13. Though reader-response theories have helped us understand and explain how we relate to the text, they do not do so fully. In reader-response theories the text is central or, at least, the person is always seen in relation to the text. In our appropriation of biblical stories the text disappears as an element per se leaving them always mediated through the need and usage of Hispanic women. For an overview of reader-response theories see Jane P.

Tompkins, *Reader-Response Criticism* (Baltimore: Johns Hopkins University Press, 1980).

14. My mother's understanding that to struggle is to live, *la vida es la lucha,* expresses this sense of ongoing resistance as a good and effective strategy in our struggle.

15. For an excellent exposition on this subject see Sharon Welch, *A Feminist Ethic of Risk* (Minneapolis: Fortress Press, 1990), 74–81.

16. Because of space constraints I cannot amplify here what this "doing theology," including biblical exegesis, in community would look like. See Isasi-Díaz and Tarango, *Hispanic Women,* particularly chapter 5.

17. For another perspective on ecumenism from a Hispanic viewpoint see Justo González, *Mañana: Christian Theology from a Hispanic Perspective* (Nashville: Abingdon Press, 1990), 55–74; also the Foreword to that book, written by Virgilio Elizondo.

18. For the task those who have privileges are called to, see chapter 5 above, "Solidarity: Love of Neighbor in the Twenty-First Century," pp. 86–104.

19. Teresa L. Amott and Julie A. Matthaei, *Race, Gender & Work* (Boston: South End Press, 1991), 346–48.

20. To the accusation that this places us in the neo-orthodox ranks, we answer that Hispanic women have not been part of the "modern experiment"; that the kind of belief in the divine that for the enlightened, scientific mind signifies lack of autonomous, critical, rational thought for us is a concrete experience that we can use as a key element in the struggle for liberation. See Christine Gudorf, "Liberation Theology's Use of Scripture: A Response to First World Critics," in *Interpretation: A Journal of Bible and Theology* (January 1987): 12–13.

21. For a thorough explanation of the relationship between liberation and salvation see Gustavo Gutiérrez, *A Theology of Liberation* (Maryknoll, N.Y.: Orbis Books, 1988), 83–105. See also Isasi-Díaz and Tarango, *Hispanic Women,* and Ada María Isasi-Díaz, *En la Lucha: Elaborating a Mujerista Theology* (Minneapolis: Fortress Press, 1992).

22. If we do not have a say, there is no doubt that the Bible will be imposed as the only or the definitive revelation of God to the exclusion of the ongoing revelation of God in our lives and the revelation of God in non-Christian religions.

23. Latinas who belong to the mainline Protestant churches use the Bible much more than do Catholic Latinas, but following the tradition of mainline Protestant churches, their approach to the Bible is not a fundamentalist one.

24. I believe dialogue among Hispanic women who interpret, appropriate, and use the Bible in very different ways is possible if we are able

to meet without the interference of priests and pastors. This has been my experience, necessarily limited.

25. For a fuller discussion of conscientization see Isasi-Díaz and Tarango, *Hispanic Women*, 94–110. Justo González's understanding of how the Bible should be read and used is along the lines we present here. I do not believe, however, that we are saying the same thing, though we do not contradict each other. See González, *Mañana,*, 75–87.

26. Juan Luis Segundo, *The Liberation of Theology* (Maryknoll, N.Y.: Orbis Books, 1982), 121.

27. Charles Curran, *Catholic Moral Theology in Dialogue* (Notre Dame: Fides Publishers, 1972), 70.

28. This section is part of an essay entitled "*Mujeristas:* A Name of Our Own," in Marc H. Ellis and Otto Maduro, eds., *The Future of Liberation Theology* (Maryknoll, N.Y.: Orbis Books, 1989), 410–19.

29. Dianne Bergant, "Exodus as a Paradigm in Feminist Theology," in Bas van Iersel and Anton Weiler, eds., *Exodus: A Lasting Paradigm,* Concilium (Edinburgh: T. & T. Clark, 1987), 100–106.

30. Much of the material in Exodus comes from the J source. P provides a framework for the J material, while E has been used to supplement J. The core of the material of the pericope here examined comes from the supplementary source, E. Supplemental material has to have some significance, whether literary, historical, or theological, for it to be considered worth adding. That the compilers/editors of the present text added this pericope would indicate that in some way it is intrinsic to the history, the theme, and the theological understanding of the exodus.

31. "The two midwives have apparently Semitic names. Puah may mean 'splendid one' or perhaps 'girl.'...Shiphrah appears...on a list of Egyptian slaves and means 'fair one'" (Brevard S. Childs, *The Book of Exodus* [Philadelphia: Westminster, 1974], 8–12).

32. J. Cheryl Exum, "'You Shall Let Every Daughter Live': A Study of Exodus 1:8–2:10," *Semeia* 28 (1983): 3–82.

33. "The attribute *Hebrew* applied here to the midwives represents the first use in Exodus of this term, which is due to recur a number of times in the continuation of the Book.... The word in question signifies in general people who were aliens in their environment, and were mostly employed as servants or slaves. In Egyptians texts, the aforementioned Egyptian term refers to enslaved people, who were compelled to do forced labour in the service of the pharaoh. In the Bible the children of Israel, or their ancestors, are called *Hebrews* particularly when the writer has in mind the relationship to the foreign environment in which they find themselves....Here, in Exodus, whilst the children of Israel are still free men [*sic*], they are called by their honoured designation, *children of Israel,* even when pharaoh speaks of them (v. 9). But after the commencement of their servitude, they are

usually referred to as *Hebrews*" (U. Cassuto, *A Commentary on the Book of Exodus* [Jerusalem: Magnum Press, Hebrew University, 1967], 13).

34. Phyllis Trible, "Depatriarchalizing in Biblical Interpretation," *JAAR*, 41 (1973): 34.

35. Childs, *Exodus*, 16.

36. Exum, "You Shall Let," 72.

37. Ibid.

38. Samuel Terrien, "Fear," in *The Interpreter's Dictionary of the Bible*, vol. 2, ed. Emory Steven Bucke (New York: Abingdon, 1962), 257.

39. Ibid., 258–59.

40. Verses 18–19 relate the confrontation between the pharaoh and the midwives. Pharaoh has ordered them directly, and therefore he is the one to whom they have to report. Because they have defied his direct order, their defiance is a direct action against him. But their defiance in the form of noncompliance is so clever that the best the pharaoh can do is to reword his order and impose it in general upon everyone. Therefore, from now on the pharaoh will find it all the more impossible to hold anyone accountable for not following his orders.

41. Ibid., 74.

42. Ibid.

43. I am most grateful to Angela Bauer for her scholarly critique of this paper.

On the Birthing Stool

Mujerista Liturgy

LAS HERMANAS is a twenty-year-old national Hispanic
women's organization that promotes justice for Hispanic
women and our communities in church and society and enables the development of leadership of Hispanic women.
Started by Chicana women in Catholic religious communities in 1971, LAS HERMANAS soon welcomed lay
women and Hispanic women from many different national
backgrounds. Given the marginality and scarcity of finan-
cial resources of Hispanic women, lack of funds has kept
the organization from carrying out its task as fully as its
members have wished. The first half of the 1980s was particularly difficult for the organization. When a group of
about one hundred of its members met in 1986 in Denver
to celebrate the fifteenth anniversary of the organization
(*la quinceañera*), key leaders in the group committed themselves to finding ways to strengthen the organization. In
the fall of 1989 a national conference was held in San
Antonio in which more than two hundred women participated. The conference was a celebration of the ability

An earlier version of this chapter was published in Marjorie Procter-Smith and
Janet R. Walton, eds., *Women at Worship* (Louisville: Westminster/John Knox Press,
1993), pp. 191–210. Used by permission of Westminster/John Knox Press.

of LAS HERMANAS to survive. It was also a celebration of the increasing number of grassroots Hispanic women who believe in the organization. The conference also provided LAS HERMANAS with an opportunity to analyze the issue of power: How has power been used to oppress us? How do we reconceptualize power so it becomes enablement and encouragement instead of control and domination? What power do we have as Hispanic women and how do we claim it as important, as life-giving? What organizational power does LAS HERMANAS have? How do we use it and strengthen it?

Since the second half of the 1970s, LAS HERMANAS has struggled with the issue of celebrating Mass as part of its conferences and meetings. The issue is not lack of belief in the Eucharist but the exclusion of women from ordained ministry in the Catholic Church. Celebration of Mass would require bringing in a male priest, something many of us find disempowering. From having Mass as a part of the conference schedule, usually with Hispanic women very actively involved in leadership, including giving the homily, the organization has moved to having a "liturgy" prepared by us, one in which only women have leadership roles.[1] "Liturgy," therefore, in our conferences means a Hispanic women's liturgy in which we celebrate in an autochthonous way who we are, our struggles, our preferred future, and our belief in the divine, in Jesus as a friend and *compañero* in the struggle. For many of us these liturgies are eucharistic; for others they are a prayer service. The goal of the organizers of the LAS HERMANAS Conferences during most of the past decade has been not to force anyone to accept our liturgies as Eucharist but rather to enable the participants to develop and experience new forms of liturgical expressions.

It was against this background that at the LAS HER-

MANAS Conference in 1989 we celebrated the "liturgy" that I am using as the framework for articulating some principle elements of *mujerista* liturgical celebrations, elements not necessarily unique but distinctively ours. This liturgy and the articulation of these principles are indeed a birthing moment, a climbing onto the birthing stool to articulate religious understandings embodied in our Hispanic women's liturgies.

A *Mujerista* Liturgy

Preparación

Four elements were important in preparing our *mujerista* liturgy: two of us were responsible for designing the liturgy;[2] those of us preparing the liturgy were part of the community gathering for the conference; the liturgical celebration was not the only ritual we had during the conference; the liturgy was understood and conceptualized as an integral part of the conference so its goals were the same as those of the conference.

In LAS HERMANAS we value teamwork and reject hierarchical structures. Very early in the history of the organization we moved from having a president, vice-president, and so forth, to a team of national coordinators. We have a small working board, and at its meetings national coordinators as well as staff participate fully in decision-making. So when it came time to plan the liturgy, it was natural to ask two of us to be responsible for preparing it. We both knew we were expected to (and we wanted to) consult with many of the other persons preparing the conference. This was not a perfunctory kind of consultation; their views carried as much weight as ours.

As Hispanic women ourselves, and because both of us responsible for designing the liturgy had worked with grassroots Hispanic women for many years, we were not strangers to those gathering for the conference. We were all part of the community of Hispanic women — a group of women rich in diversity whose ethnicity works as a common denominator.[3] Besides, between us we knew personally about two-thirds of those coming to the conference. More than half of the conference participants were grassroots Hispanic women, women at the lower end of the economic ladder who work at manual labor and who have limited formal education. The rest of the participants were professional women with relative economic security and a college or graduate education.

Because as *mujeristas* we value rituals, we had decided to use a variety of them at this conference. As has become traditional for LAS HERMANAS, our conference started with an opening ritual telling our organizational story. This time, rather than the "regular" opening prayer service, we used audio-visuals that were very effective. We then had a wonderful one-woman show: a Hispanic actress did a series of vignettes that put us in touch with and celebrated our tradition of struggle as Hispanic women. A second moment of ritual in the conference was our Saturday night *fiesta*, also a traditional event at our national conferences. This *fiesta* is an evening of celebrating those who have served the organization; it provides a rare opportunity for Hispanic women who are gifted as singers, dancers, poets, and comedians to perform in a safe, welcoming environment. Finally, the *fiesta* is a wonderful time of just having fun, enjoying each other and celebrating.

Since these other two rituals had served to accomplish some of the goals of the conference, the liturgy did not have to carry an undue burden within the design of the conference. We had established from the very beginning that rituals were an important element of the conference and were key in our attempt to communicate ideas, values, and a vision of our preferred future. Little by little, from the beginning, through rituals, lectures, and group discussion the conference had unfolded the announced theme: power. When the time arrived for the closing liturgy, we had done our analysis of power and had set out strategies on how to proceed. Analyzing and determining strategies are in themselves empowering processes. Even so, though we hoped that the whole conference had achieved this goal, we depended on the liturgy to help the women feel empowered to face the daily struggle for survival with new understandings and renewed strength.

Ambiente y Símbolos

Several understandings and convictions guide us *mujeristas* in determining the setting for our liturgies. First, it is important for us to claim and affirm as sacred the place where we meet. As Hispanic women often we are treated as if we possess a diminished humanity; therefore, it is critical for us to claim as sacred any space where we meet to celebrate ourselves and our struggles and to recommit ourselves to *la lucha* (the struggle). It is an important way of asserting our participation in the holiness of God, for as Hispanic women we are made in the image and likeness of the divine.

The *ambiente* (environment) for our liturgies, wherever they are held, has to remind us of the sacred spaces that many of us carve out even in the humblest of houses. Regardless of economic level, degree of formal education, or type of job we have, the vast majority of Hispanic women have altars in our homes, or at least pictures of Mary, Jesus, and/or the saints hanging on the walls. Our home altars are full of statues and are a tangible way of making the divine present. It is at home altars that God's presence is invoked, where mutual commitment and responsibility between us and God are established. Our home altars clearly indicate that for us the divine is directly accessible; that we do not have to depend on priests or pastors to relate to the divine.[4]

So for this liturgy, in the center of the room where we had spent most of the conference, we set up an altar like the ones many of us have at home. We had asked conference participants to bring statues or pictures of women who had been significant in their lives. We placed on the altar all that they brought: statues of Mary, the mother of Jesus, represented in different ways; pictures of mothers, grandmothers, sisters, women friends, daughters, nieces, granddaughters; holy cards of women saints; and figures of women dear to their owners because of their artistic or some other value.

We also placed candles on the altar. Candles are always present in Hispanic rituals for they carry out three important functions. First, candles stand for us in the presence of God. We light our candles and then go our way, confident that our burning candles represent us before God. Second, candles are an offering to the divine that even the poor can afford. Candles are lit not only to remind God of us but also to thank God for helping us and as an act of praise to the divine. Third, the warmth and light of the candle remind us of the hearth — the center of the home for Hispanic women, the place that incarnates the deep sense of hospitality which we consider "a test of ... [our] closeness to God."[5] As we shall see below, candles were on the altar not only because of their symbolic value but also because they played an important role in the ritual.

We also placed on the altar bread, chalices containing

milk and honey, and dates. Though we wanted to use bread because of its centrality in Christian eucharistic celebrations, we wanted bread to be seen also as food for the road, as sustenance for the struggle ahead of us. That is why we also included dates, which had been brought to the conference by a grassroots women's group from California. To complete the meal we needed something to drink, but we did not want to use wine for two reasons. First, we were not trying in any way to have a Mass or to imitate the Mass. Second, and perhaps more important, wine is not a common drink among Hispanic women. We decided to use milk and honey. Even though it is uncommon among us, we believed we could imbue it with a symbolism to which the women could relate. We talked during the ritual of the milk our women-bodies produce to sustain life; we explained how the Israelites talked about their preferred future as the land flowing with milk and honey. It was in this sense that milk and honey represented the abiding presence of God with us and among us: it helped us celebrate our women-bodies and to keep always present before us the preferred future for which we struggle.

One more symbol was very important for us: the circle. We wanted to symbolize that we are all equals around the altar, that our liturgies are expressions of a community of faith struggling for liberation. So we symbolized equality and unity by being around the altar in a circle. Since there were several women who could not sit on the floor, we set a circle of chairs for them while the rest of the participants sat on the floor.

Palabra y Canto

Because we come from an oral tradition our usage of *palabra* (word) is not a matter of reading a prepared text;

words arise from the participants as an expression of who they are, a relating of their lived-experiences. For us the most important use of words is in song. For the LAS HERMANAS Conference in 1989, we were gifted with Rosa Marta Zárate Macías, a *cantadora,* a composer and singer who considers what she does a vocation and who understands her musical talents to be an instrument in the struggle for the liberation of our people. For this liturgy we used three of her songs, well known to most of us, songs that deal with the central message of our liturgy.[6]

A second use of words was the Bible reading and the sermon. For this we used two guidelines. First, we used a biblical text that would provide a "reality check" for Hispanic women. Often what we do is diminished, ignored, or misunderstood. So one of the main roles the Bible plays for us is to help us know that what we have done, what has happened to us, and what we think are not wrong. Women in the Bible who struggle have lived through the same kind of experience. These texts are salvific for us because they become an effective instrument in our struggle for liberation. Second, the preaching had to be dialogic and engaging, providing women with an opportunity to hear their own voices in this sacred ritual. The homily must not be an attempt to give a single interpretation of a biblical text but rather to enable each one present to do her own articulation, trusting that because there is enough commonality in our lived-experience and because we are all involved in the struggle for liberation, common themes will emerge from the rich variety of articulations. Of course during a short dialogued homily this process cannot be completed, but this was the intention that guided the homily in our service. This not only affected what was said but also the way it was said.[7]

This same principle guided us in two other uses of words

during the ritual. During the first part of the liturgy we wanted to lift up the power of the women represented by the images and pictures on our altar. We asked participants to call out the names of powerful women in their lives. This name-calling grew in intensity and created a wonderful wave of power in the room. Later in the liturgy, when we asked women to call out the names they give Mary, the Mother of Jesus, the name-calling became like a soft chant, a reverential litany, expressing love and care.

After the dialogued homily came the blessing of the food we were to share. We wanted every woman to participate in this blessing but did not think that everybody reading a common text would be conducive to ownership of what was being said. Therefore, we developed a "blessing prayer" in Spanish and English, with seven strophes, each finishing with a short line to be repeated by all of us.[8]

Facilitadoras

Because one of the main objectives of *mujerista* theology is the enablement of moral agency of Hispanic women, our understanding of leadership is that of facilitation and empowerment. An intrinsic part of this understanding is to have a multiplicity of leaders. There are three reasons for this. First, we want our liturgies to provide opportunity for as many women as possible to have an active role in sacred rituals in order to counter their exclusion from approaching the altar during worship in their churches. Second, we believe that leadership is a function of the community vested in a person for a given function because of her gifts. Leadership is not a permanent state of a few. The development of leadership qualities inherent in many Hispanic women is an important strategy in our struggle for liberation. Third, multiplicity of leaders helps decentralize power. Sharing power means that those who design a liturgy have to let go of it, have to trust it into the hands of others in the community who can, and do, modify it in order to have their voices heard.

We wanted, therefore, as many Hispanic women as possible to have a leadership role in the liturgy. Twenty-five women served in that capacity. This gave us a sense that our liturgical celebration was not so much a distribution of bread but a gathering of the fragments of the bread of the lives of many women — a sharing that was to bring pride in who we are and joy because of our faithfulness to the struggle and to our communities.

Texto y Secuencia

Following is the text and sequence of the Hispanic Women's Liturgy celebrated at the LAS HERMANAS Conference in San Antonio on October 28, 1989.

Opening Ritual

Those who have a leadership role in the liturgy sit in silence. As the rest of the women come into the room they become aware of the silent atmosphere and join in it. Once the gathered community is ready, one by one different women go to the altar, light a candle, and while holding it on high say one of the following lines.[9]

The power to give life.
The power of being vulnerable without being weak.

The power of believing in a better future.
The power of changing oppressive situations.
The power to face difficult circumstances.
The power of not giving up.
The power of loving and claiming the need for love.
The power of crying.
The power that is ours because we are women.[10]

The community is invited to name the powerful women they have known, who have influenced them, while the rest of the candles on the table are lit by two women.[11]

Once all the candles are lit another woman says:

This space in which we have spent these three days is full of the light of our power. We know we are blessed by God and by Mary. Let us call out the different names we give her.

Pause for the women to invoke Mary. Once they have finished, a different woman says the following.

And now I ask you to turn to the person on your right and bless her using whatever words and gestures you want.[12]

When the women are almost finished blessing each other, the song starts.

Lucha, Poder, y Esperanza

Lucha, Poder, Esperanza	Struggle, power, hope
Mujer Hispana en tu vientre	Hispanic woman in your womb
llevas semillas del Verbo.	you carry seeds of the Word.
¡Demos vida al continente!	Let's give life to the continent.
Adelante compañeras	Onward, *compañeras*
que a nuestro pueblo asesinan	they are murdering our people
y a la tierra nuestra madre	and our mother, the earth,
el imperio ultraja y viola.	the empire is ravaging and raping.

Vamos a unirnos, hermanas *firmes, valientes, ya basta* *de ser esclavas del miedo* *hijas de raza violada.*	Let us come together, sisters firmly, bravely, it is enough! No longer slaves of fear we'll be nor daughters of a raped race.
Al viento nadie lo para *al mar nadie lo encadena* *las mujeres solidarias* *son fuego que nadie apaga.*	No one stops the wind, no one chains the sea, the women in solidarity are a fire no one can extinguish.
Tu causa es causa del Pueblo, *tu dignidad es sagrada* *mujer color de la tierra* *árbol de la vida nueva.*	Your cause is the people's cause your dignity is sacred woman, your color is the earth's you are tree of new life.
Lucha, poder, esperanza *sea consigna en la batalla* *por rescatar la justicia* *nuestra hermana aprisionada.*	Struggle, power, hope may it be the cry of our struggle to rescue justice our imprisoned sister.

La Palabra entre Nosotras (the word of God among us)

A reading of Exodus 1:15–21 is followed by a dialogued homily — to last about ten minutes built around the following points. The homilist walks around among the women gathered.

1. The homilist asks if there are any midwives present. Who was helped by a midwife to give birth? What was her name? Call on as many women as want to speak.

2. The homilist gives thoughts on the close relationship between women and giving life.

3. She talks about the need for us to ask ourselves what kind of life we want for our children.

4. She asks, What did Shiphrah and Puah do? Could they speak back to the pharaoh and say, "We will not

do that"? What was more important, to voice their convictions or to find a way to save the children?

5. She presents thoughts on the value of planning strategies, of keeping the goal of liberation in mind, of doing things together and not alone, the value of analyzing what we can accomplish, given the fact that we are oppressed.

6. She asks, What is the central theme of the book of Exodus? Who is the main character? Without the women at the beginning of the Exodus story, the main event, the liberation of the people, would not have happened. The midwives were a role model for Moses, of how he should act when he faced pharaoh, how not to give in, how always to keep in mind the liberation of the people.

Blessing Prayer

Each stanza is read by a different woman from where she is in the circle. Everybody repeats the last line of each stanza.

The power of the seed from which the wheat grows.
El poder de la semilla de la que surge el trigo.
El poder de la semilla.

The power of the earth nurtures the seed and makes it flourish.
El poder de la tierra que nutre la semilla y la hace brotar.
El poder de la tierra.

The power of the sun that gives warmth and light to the wheat.
El poder del sol que le da luz y calor al trigo.
El poder del sol.

The power of the *campesinas, campesinos,* who care for and harvest the wheat.

El poder de las campesinas, los campesinos, que cuidan del trigo y lo cosechan.

El poder de las campesinas.

The power of the yeast that even if it is small in quantity makes all the dough to rise.

El poder de la levadura que aunque mínima en cantidad hace que la masa se alce.

El poder de la levadura.

The power of the bread which sustains us and without which there is no life.

El poder del pan que nos sustenta y sin él no hay vida.

El poder del pan.

One of the campesina women goes to the altar, lifts the bread over her head, and breaks the loaf.

The power of this community which in breaking this bread renews its commitment to the people who struggle for their liberation.

El poder de esta comunidad que en el partir del pan renueva su compromiso con el pueblo que lucha por su liberación.

El poder de esta comunidad.

Another woman goes to the altar and lifting the cup says the following:

This is the milk which comes from our bodies and nourishes life. It is mixed with honey, for milk and honey was the symbol for our ancestors of the promised land, of a better future, of liberation. We bless it by drinking of it for it will sustain us in the struggle.

Another woman helps the woman at the altar finish breaking the bread. They set several stations around the table
with cups, baskets with bread, and plates with dates. Then
she says:

> The gifts of God for the people of God, come and eat
> joyfully, with the resolution and understanding that
> we will continue in the struggle and that God will
> always sustain us if we sustain one another. Come
> and feast.

While the people go to the table and feed themselves
we sing.

PROFETIZA

Profetiza, pueblo mío	Prophesy, my people
Profetiza una vez más	Prophesy once again
Que tu voz sea el eco del clamor	May your voice be the clamor
De los pueblos en la opresión	Of oppressed peoples
Profetiza pueblo, hispano	Prophesy, Hispanic people
Profetiza una vez más	Prophesy once again
Anunciándoles a los pobres	Announcing to the poor
Una nueva sociedad.	A new society.

1. *Profeta te consagro*
   No haya duda y temor
   En tu andar por la historia
   Sé fiel a tu misión.

   I consecrate you prophet
   Let there be no doubt nor fear
   As you walk through history
   Be faithful to your mission.

2. *Anúnciales a los pueblos*
   Que Dios renovará
   Su pacto en la justicia
   Su amor florecerá.

   Announce to the peoples
   That God will renovate
   God's justice-covenant
   God's love will flourish.

3. *Denuncia todo aquello*
   Que causa la opresión
   Para que se convierta
   Y vuelva de nuevo a Dios.

   Denounce everything
   That causes oppression
   So that it can be converted
   And return once again to God.

4. *Esta sea tu esperanza*   May this be your hope
   Esta sea tu misión   May this be your mission
   Ser constructor del Reino   Be a builder of the Reign
   Sociedad del Amor.   A society of love.

5. *Es hora de mi gracia*   This is the hour of my grace
   Sacramento de Dios   Sacrament of God
   Sé signo de mi alianza   Be a sign of my covenant
   Sé luz de un nuevo sol.   Be the light of a new sun.[13]

Closing Ritual

Several women step up to the altar and pull from underneath the table balls of ribbons that have been tied to the legs of the table. They throw them to the congregation, asking each to hold on to the ribbon that reaches her and pass the end on to the person next to her. One of the women says:

> These ribbons are a symbol of our lives and of our renewed commitment to the struggle. Allow these ribbons to connect us and unite us.

Pause until all are holding the ribbons.

> Now let us cut a piece of this ribbon and take it with us to remember that we are not alone in the struggle.

Scissors are passed out. While they are cutting the ribbons the final song starts. Women on the outskirts of the circle throw confetti and *serpentina* (paper carnival ribbons) into the middle.

Cántico de Mujer

Bendita mujer	Blessed is the woman
La que sabe ser fiel	Who knows how to be faithful
Al quehacer de implantar	To the work of planting
La justicia y la paz;	Justice and peace;
Dichosa será	Happy will be
La mujer que hace opción	The woman who makes an option
Por la causa de Dios	For God's cause
Por la ley del amor.	For the law of love.

1. *Hoy canto al Dios del pueblo en mi guitarra*
   Today I sing to the God of my people with my guitar
   Un canto de mujer que se libera
   A song of a woman who liberates herself
   Dios se solidariza con mi causa
   God is in solidarity with my cause
   Me consagra portador de la esperanza
   Consecrates me bearer of hope.
   Dios escuchó el clamor de nuestro pueblo
   God heard the cries of our people
   Se alió al empobrecido y explotado
   Is an ally of the impoverished and the exploited
   Y a la mujer libera de cadenas
   And frees women from her chains
   Impuestas con crueldad por tantos siglos.
   Imposed with cruelty for so many centuries.

2. *Harás justicia a todas las mujeres*
   You will make justice a reality for all women
   Que firmes no cayeron ante el yugo
   Who were firm and did not fall when faced with the yoke
   Nos das la libertad y reivindicas
   You give us freedom and revindicate
   O Dios tu semejanza originaria
   O God your original likeness.

Al mal pastor que causa tanto daño
  To the bad pastor who has caused so much damage
Al gobernante infiel que vende al pueblo
  To the unfaithful ruler who sells the people
A todo quien oprime tu destruyese
  You destroy all who oppress
Sin piedad del poder tu los derrumbas
  Without mercy you dethrone them from their power.

3. *Nos llamas a gestar en nuestro vientre*
     You call us to gestate in our womb
  Mujeres y hombres nuevos, pueblos fuertes
     New women and men, a strong people
  Nos unges servidoras, profetisas
     You anoint us servants, prophets
  Testigos de tu amor que nos redime
     Witnesses of your redeeming love.
  Has puesto en mi cantar una esperanza
     You have put in my song a note of hope
  Seré eco de tu amor que reconcilia
     I will be an echo of your reconciling love
  Espada de dos filos sea mi canto
     May my song be a two-edged sword
  Pregón de un evangelio libertario
     A proclamation of your liberating gospel.[14]

Analysis and Critique

As mentioned above, the goal of this conference and of the liturgy was the empowerment of Hispanic women and a celebration of the power of LAS HERMANAS to survive. Those of us responsible for designing the liturgy wanted to provide an experience of celebration of Hispanic women's selves, their commitments, their struggles; we saw the celebration as an affirmation of ourselves that would help us in our *lucha*. At the end of the last song, there was no doubt that we had succeeded. The mood was festive, joyful; there were tears that revealed the depth of the experience we had just had. Women milled around for a long time, embracing each other, saying endlessly, "¡Gracias!" to those of us who had prepared the conference and the liturgy.

In the general design of the conference, we saw the liturgy as a teaching moment in two respects. First, it provided an experience of a different kind of celebration to which the majority of Hispanic women have no access. We know that different elements of the ritual have been adapted and used repeatedly by those who participated in the original liturgy. Having a different liturgical experience has provided them with a point of comparison they can use to judge and critique liturgies in their own churches. Second, the reading from Exodus, the homily, the litanies, and the prayer of blessing as well as the words of the songs were important teaching texts. They presented theological understandings and strategies for the daily struggle of those who participated in the conference.

We wanted in a special way to make grassroots women feel at home. For some of them this was the first time they stayed in a hotel, the first time they were in a conference with only women, the first time they heard a woman preach, the first time it was one of them who broke the bread.[15] We were very happy at how well we were able to "translate" the home altar into an altar for a ritual for two hundred people. It was the sense of home altar that brought the elements of the liturgy together and helped many of the participants feel very comfortable in surroundings quite different from their own.

We intended to use the liturgy to demystify the sacred, for the mystification of the sacred is a control mechanism used by "religious professionals." We wanted to enable Hispanic women to understand that if we believe God became human in the person of Jesus, all of us, not only priests and pastors, participate in the divine. We believe we accomplished this, particularly for the Hispanic women who had a leadership role in the liturgy.

Hispanic *mestiza* and *mulata* Christianity is a mixture of religious understandings and practices brought over by the *conquistadores* and the priests that accompanied them with religious understandings and practices of the Amerindian world they ransacked and those of the Africans they brought over as slaves. Though some of the popular religious practices we used in the liturgy, such as the home altar, statues, and candles, have Amerindian and African influences, our liturgy did not include significant Amerindian and African elements. This is something that we have to tend to in future liturgies.

Para Terminar

Since 1978 LAS HERMANAS has given great attention to rituals. Part of this has to do with how important rituals are for us as Hispanic women. Outward expressions of who we are, what we believe, how we feel, are a key element of our culture. As a matter of fact, one of the great hardships we find in being in a Euro-American culture is the unacceptability of expressing genuine emotions. Rituals such as this liturgy become vehicles, then, for being our most authentic selves. These *mujerista* liturgies are indeed opportunities for self-affirmation; they are moments that fill us with hope since, during our liturgies, we are able to give free rein to our way of being; they are moments of celebration of our preferred future in which our ethnicity is not an impediment but a fundamental element of the soci-

ety in which we live. *Mujerista* liturgies help us give birth
to ourselves as liberated Hispanic women.

Notes

1. Even today this is not totally without problems for some of the
participants. What LAS HERMANAS has done for its last two conferences is to list or announce the schedule of Masses for Sunday in a nearby
church. We have never discussed openly why we do not have Mass as part
of the program. The silence around this issue is not because of the differences among Hispanic women but because an open discussion would
become known to the Hispanic hierarchy and clergy and result in difficulty
for the work of the organization.

2. Maria Antonietta Berriozábal and I were the two women who took
responsibility for designing the liturgy.

3. Ethnicity here is not just an identification of country of origin
but refers to the present socio-economic-political-ethnic reality of Hispanic
women in this country. For a fuller description of this concept of ethnicity
see Ada María Isasi-Díaz, *En la Lucha — Elaborating a Mujerista Theology*
(Minneapolis: Fortress Press, 1993).

4. C. Gilbert Romero, *Hispanic Devotional Piety* (Maryknoll, N.Y.:
Orbis Books, 1991), 83–97. See also Ada María Isasi-Díaz and Yolanda
Tarango, *Hispanic Women: Prophetic Voice in the Church* (San Francisco:
Harper and Row, 1988; reprint Minneapolis: Fortress Press, 1992), 37–38.

5. Ibid., 84.

6. Text of the three songs below in the "Text and Sequence" section.

7. More about this when we discuss the role of leadership in Hispanic
women's liturgies.

8. The idea for the format of the "blessing prayer" and some of
the content are from Carter Heyward, "Blessing the Bread (A Litany for
Four Voices)" in *Prayers and Poem • Songs and Stories — Ecumenical Decade
1988–1998: Churches in Solidarity with Women* (Geneva: World Council of
Churches Publications, 1988), 79–80.

9. Some of the women chose to say their line in Spanish; some said it
in English.

10. Several women at this point decided to add their own statement to
the litany.

11. Some of the leaders had been cued to start and also to call out
names while other people were doing so in order to create the effect we

wanted instead of a one-name-after-the-other approach. There were at least twenty small "vigil" candles on the table.

12. Though we had intended for each woman to bless only one or two of the people closest to them, many took it upon themselves to bless many of the women in the room.

13. Rosa Marta Zárate Macías, *Profetiza y Cántico de Mujer* (Chicago: GIA Publications, 1991), sound cassette. Used with permission.

14. Zárate Macías, sound cassette. Used with permission.

15. There was one man present, a very supportive Roman Catholic priest who has come to our last two conferences and who participates fully in a very low-key way. He is on leave from the diocese of San Bernardino after being dismissed from his job by the bishop because of the radicalness and effectiveness of his work.

Rituals and *Mujeristas'* Struggle for Liberation

Mujerista theology is a liberative praxis — reflective action that has as its goal the liberation of Hispanic women. Using as its source the lived experience of Hispanic women, *mujerista* theology seeks to be a platform for our voices as we reflect upon and articulate our religious understandings and practices. As a communal theological praxis *mujerista* theology endeavors to enable Hispanic women to be agents of our own history, to enhance our moral agency, and to design and participate in actions that are effective ways of struggling for survival. It is within this framework that one needs to look at *mujerista* liturgies.

Principles and Understandings of *Mujerista* Liturgies

Mujerista liturgies exist in many forms and take place in many venues and circumstances, though most of the time they are not recognized as liturgies. For us, *mujerista*

An earlier version of this essay was published as "*Mujerista* Liturgies and the Struggle for Liberation" in Louis-Marie Chauvet and François Kabasele Lumbala, eds., *Liturgy and the Body*, Concilium 1995/3 (Maryknoll, N.Y.: Orbis Books, 1995), 104–11.

liturgies happen when Hispanic women's lived experiences constitute the source of a celebration and when that celebration contributes effectively to our liberation.[1] *Mujerista* liturgies are powerful means for Hispanic women to understand and articulate our religious beliefs. *Mujerista* liturgies provide us with opportunities to express and strengthen our values as a community of faith struggling for liberation. In our liturgies we affirm our willingness to risk. *Mujerista* liturgies provide for us an opportunity to share experiences, celebrate the small victories we have, and encourage one other.

For *mujeristas* our liturgies are communal celebrations, rituals that actively enable us to forge empowering relationships and at the same time help us to have control over our lives.[2] Our liturgies are hope-providing moments in the daily struggle for survival; they are signs of rebellion, for when the oppressed celebrate, we are telling the oppressor that we have not given up, that we have not been conquered.

Mujerista liturgies stand as a critique and a denunciation of institutional liturgies which, whether consciously or not, function mainly to maintain the good order of patriarchy. They are ritual attempts to subvert and transform "precisely those spiritual and social relational schemes of traditional liturgies that are believed to constitute good order."[3] Yet, our liturgies are consistent with the best of the faith tradition in which most of us are rooted, Roman Catholicism. *Mujeristas* believe, as Medellín said, that any liturgical celebration "crowns and implies a commitment to the human situation, to development and human promotion."[4]

Our insistence on the lived-experience of Hispanic women as a source of *mujeristas'* liturgies is based on two principles advanced in the Constitution on the Sacred Liturgy of Vatican II. First, liturgical celebrations must communicate God's presence and celebrate the identity of the people gathered; second, as symbolic activity liturgical presentations must help to bring about an experience of individual and communal transformation.[5]

In many ways *mujerista* liturgies amplify and expand rituals already at the heart of Hispanic popular religion. Marginalized as it is within the USA, Hispanic culture is always being threatened with extinction. For us popular religion is one of the key elements of our Hispanic ethnicity. It is a means of self-identification. When we insist on it, we are claiming it as part of the struggle to exist in our own particular way within a very dominant and elitist culture. It is popular religion that constitutes for us "a system of symbols which acts to establish powerful, pervasive, and long-lasting moods and motivations ... by formulating conceptions of general order of existence and clothing these conceptions with such an aura of factuality that the moods and motivations seems uniquely realistic."[6]

Many symbols of popular religion at the heart of *mujerista* liturgies arise from medieval Spanish Catholic devotional piety and from the African and Amerindian faith practices of our ancestors. They also arise from the rituals of a significant number of our sisters and brothers in Latin America and the Caribbean and in our communities in the USA. These symbols often take on meanings different from the original ones, gathered as they are from the three religious traditions that root Hispanic popular religion. These symbols go hand in hand with beliefs, attitudes, and values. Therefore, our popular religion is actually a religious subculture, for it is a way of thinking and acting not of individuals but of Hispanics as a group of persons. As such it is transmitted as an intrinsic element of our culture.

Thus, for *mujerista* liturgies we do not need to go far to

find liberating symbols and ritual schemes. In our own popular religion we have a rich "complex of symbolic practices, discursive and non-discursive, enacted in ritual drama and materialized in visual images," readily available.[7] However, we do not gather them indiscriminately. Using a liberative lens, *mujeristas* recognize that popular religion has its failings and ambiguities; it too contains elements that contribute directly or indirectly to legitimize the oppression of Hispanic women. Some of those nonliberating elements are fatalism, superstition, and the glorification of suffering. Elements of this kind we certainly reject. But liberating elements of popular religion — such as availability of the divine in our daily and ordinary lives, direct access to the divine, nonclerical leadership — these we certainly embrace and use widely in *mujerista* liturgies. They provide us with a revolutionary impulse in our struggle for survival.

Mujerista Liturgies as Safe Space

In the USA Hispanic women as well as Hispanic men are in many ways aliens in the very country where we live. We find understanding and acceptance and a kind of tolerated participation in society at large as long as we "translate" ourselves into the dominant cultural norms and patterns of that society. By the sheer force of numbers, at least in certain areas of the USA, Hispanics have some impact on the dominant culture, but only in a very minute way. Often, the impact has been turned into a commercialization of our culture, which means that one can hear Hispanic music and eat Hispanic food quite readily in the USA without having any knowledge of Hispanic history, of our mores and values.

It is only when we Hispanics return to our *barrios,*

our neighborhoods, that we can be ourselves. Even there, though, women are not completely at home. Since the Hispanic culture is a patriarchal culture, Hispanic women, even in our own communities, in our own families, and in our own homes, have to continue to "translate" ourselves. Once a Hispanic woman has acquired a critical consciousness of her oppression, once she is a *mujerista,* the effort to "translate" herself is all the more demanding, all the more difficult. *Mujerista* liturgies are, in many ways, a safe space for us, providing us with the opportunity to find out about our own selves, to share freely and to celebrate how we imagine the divine and how we understand questions of ultimate meaning. *Mujerista* liturgies are free of patriarchal distortions and other forms of domination, such as ethnic prejudice, classism, and elitism. And one of the signs of how well *mujerista* liturgies achieve this goal is the fact that during our rituals Hispanic women bare their souls and share intimacies and thoughts they say they have not been able to admit before even to themselves.

For example, at the end of a national conference of Hispanic women, 150 of us gathered for a concluding *mujerista* ritual of healing. We sat on the floor around a huge basin of water that was surrounded by candles, stones, flowers, pictures of dear ones, dead and alive, and numerous holy cards of Our Lady of Guadalupe, Our Lady of Charity, Our Lady of Mt. Carmel, Our Lady of Altagracia, the Infant of Prague, the Holy Child of Atocha, the Crucified Lord of Esquipulas, St. Thérèse of Lisieux, St. Jude, St. Joseph, and others. After some moments of silence and a gathering song, the enablers of the liturgy invited us to take a stone and place it in the water, mentioning at the same time, if we so desired, a hurt from which we wanted to be cured. For over forty-five minutes the women named their hurts and asked for healing. A daughter and a mother embraced and wept after the daughter asked to be healed from her dislike of her mother. A woman said this was the first time she accepted that she needed healing in order to stop an extramarital affair in which she was involved. Another asked for healing of homophobia for herself and for all of us there. A young girl asked healing of her disgust of her fat body. A young farmworker wanted to be healed of being afraid that she might lose her job if she stood up for her rights.

The petitions for healing became a nonstoppable litany as the Hispanic women realized that they were safe, that they could say aloud what some of them had not dared to verbalize even to themselves. In many ways those women "heard" each other into speech. Furthermore, as they heard such frank prayers for the healing of such intimate hurts, these women empowered each other, nudged each other into articulating their pain. And there was no stopping them. Several times the enablers tried gently to bring this part of the liturgy to a close without success. Tears were flowing freely as Hispanic women used this ritual to reveal themselves, their failures, fears, dreams, and expectations. Here they did not have to "translate" themselves in any way. Here, in the safe space provided by this ritual, they had no need to pretend, for they were with others who accepted them even without full understanding. Here in this safe space many recovered their voices, voices silenced by the marginality that we suffer as Hispanics, and especially as Hispanic women.

Relocating the Sacred[8]

Mujerista liturgies relocate the sacred. They locate the sacred in the midst of the marginalized, of the poor and the oppressed, instead of in institutional churches that often do little or nothing to be in solidarity with Hispanic women's struggle for liberation. In so doing this, *mujeristas* claim for ourselves religious authority, the authority to make contact with the divine in our own way, according to our own experience, and using our *mujerista* selves, made in the image of God, as a metaphor for the divine. Thus *mujerista* rituals threaten the control of the divine which the churches have claimed as their exclusive possession — and quite successfully so — for many centuries.

But *mujerista* liturgies could have a wider impact if we analyzed the church from a sociological perspective. The church, from the viewpoint of religious power, is "a structured set of religious agents and institutions that, at a determinate moment, and in the religious field of a particular society, has acquired a monopoly of the legitimate exercise of religious power."[9] The church, in this sense, has the ability to confer "religious legitimacy upon an agent, a teaching, an activity, or an organization."[10] This is precisely what the patriarchal organized church does for the patriarchal systems and organizations in society that keep Hispanic women marginalized, that dominate and oppress us.

As *mujerista* liturgies relocate the sacred, wresting religious power from the church and limiting its ability to legitimate present society, our rituals begin to threaten the social cohesion of patriarchal society. Also, since *mujerista* liturgies unite Hispanic women in thought and provide for them an alternative to societal patriarchal consciousness, our rituals produce a *mística*, an intangible force that enables Hispanic women to face up to their oppressors.[11] *Mujerista* liturgies produce a *mística*, that is, a social cohesion that enables participants to do what they have not been able to do alone but that becomes possible to do with those who experience the same ritual.

An example of this happened at the Third National Hispanic Pastoral Encuentro (Gathering), which took place in
Washington, D.C., in August of 1985. The input from
the process carried on in Hispanic communities around the
country was distilled into several statements that were to
serve as the basis for a national pastoral plan for Catholic
Hispanics. None of the statements included a denunciation
of the church's unwillingness to allow women to participate fully in the church. At the first general session, where
representatives from dioceses were to vote on the proposed
statements, a new statement was introduced that had to
do with the full participation of women in the church.
Though a majority of those voting (at least 50 percent
plus 1) endorsed the new statement, the organizers claimed
to be using a consensus model and declared that a simple
majority was not therefore acceptable.

That night several of us met to decide how to proceed.
We thought it important to show that the issue of the full
participation of women in the church was not the idea of
just a minority of the people there. We decided that what
would draw the greatest number of people would be a ritual. And so we spread the word that we would gather the
next day at the steps of the National Shrine, where the
meeting was taking place, half an hour before the starting
time of the next general session. We would gather to pray.
The ritual we designed was very simple: we were to pray
the rosary aloud as we stood around a banner we happened
to have with us that had some bland saying on it. Nothing
else: just pray the rosary.

We thought we might get maybe fifty to a hundred
to participate. But at least four or five hundred, mostly
women, participated. Instead of being inside preparing to
participate in the "official" morning prayer, at least half the
participants were outside praying the rosary in protest. This

simple ritual, for so long the mainstay of Hispanic women, had successfully relocated the sacred. We had successfully limited, temporarily but in a very real way, the power of the church to legitimate what was happening at the Encuentro. The sacred was now outside with us while we prayed in protest. And it was not until we marched inside the church singing, until we brought the sacred inside with us, that the planned opening prayer inside the church was able to start.

In analyzing what happened during our ritual of protest two points are important to notice. First, as we prayed the rosary we saw women — many of whom we knew personally and who were not the kind to protest against priests and bishops — grow stronger in their demand for justice, grow angrier at the way the vote they had won was taken away from them. That anger, that strength, was what made the crowd at the end of the rosary, spontaneously and to the surprise of those of us who had organized the ritual, start singing as they marched into the church. The Hispanic women wanted to take their protest inside, to space controlled by the "official" authorities. We wanted to be sure that the ones responsible for the Encuentro realized that we were not going to allow them to ignore us, to deny us our right to voice our beliefs and to have them taken into consideration.

Second, most of the women there had participated in the national process that had yielded the statements then being proposed at the Encuentro. Yet they had not insisted on a statement on the role of women in the church. But at the national gathering, a very simple ritual had produced a *mística* that enabled the women to demand justice for ourselves. Several of the key organizers of the Encuentro repeatedly blamed a small group of us — three of us! — for what happened there. How wrong they are! There is no way that a mere three of us could have motivated and organized the women to do what they did. What was operating there was this understanding of *mística* that is generated by *mujerista* rituals. And what was the result? Though the statement that had earlier received a majority of the votes was not allowed to stand, another one, less strong but nonetheless very good, was substituted and had to be included in the Hispanic national pastoral plan signed by the Hispanic bishops. And then we must not minimize what happened personally to the women who participated in the ritual. There is no way we can measure in general the impact this experience had for all of them. But to generalize from the couple of dozen women we spoke to about it, participating in the *mujerista* ritual helped them significantly to see the oppression of women in the church and led them to determine that they would work to change such a situation.

Conclusion

Mujerista liturgies are both born out of and become expressions of Hispanic women's determination to be self-defining women. In these rituals we draw from our lived-experiences, from our needs, hopes, and expectations, to create rituals that will help us realize ever more strongly that God makes a preferential option for us because we are marginalized and oppressed. And, though the church continues to deny Hispanic women, in fact all women, full participation, *mujeristas* believe that the reappropriation of the sacred that happens through our rituals ultimately does contribute to change the social order. Our *mujerista* liturgies are wonderful and transforming. But they are also a call to us *mujeristas* to embrace the struggle; to realize that to struggle is to live.

Notes

1. Because our culture is mainly a non-secularized culture, the vast majority of celebrations organized by Hispanic women somehow link whatever is being celebrated to our understanding of the divine. In this essay, however, we refer only to those that intentionally try to make us aware of God's presence in our lives and our relationship to the divine.

2. Catherine Bell, *Ritual Theory, Ritual Practice* (New York: Oxford Press, 1992), 81–92, 123.

3. Mary Collins, "Principles of Feminist Liturgy," in Marjorie Procter-Smith and Janet R. Walton, eds., *Women at Worship* (Louisville: Westminster/John Knox Press, 1993), 19, 17–24.

4. *The Church in the Present-Day Transformation of Latin America in the Light of the Council,* Medellín Conclusions (Bogotá, Colombia: CELAM, 1971), #4.

5. The Second Vatican Council, "Constitution on the Sacred Liturgy," in Walter M. Abbott, S.J., ed., *The Documents of Vatican II* (New York: America Press, 1966), part 1.

6. Clifford Geertz, *The Interpretation of Culture* (New York: Basic Books, 1973), 90.

7. Michael R. Candelaria, *Popular Religion and Liberation* (Albany: State University of New York Press, 1990), 13.

8. I am indebted for this understanding to Sister Gay Redmond, a Ph.D. candidate in the Department of Religion and Society at Drew University, who died before she could complete her dissertation.

9. Otto Maduro, *Religion and Social Conflict* (Maryknoll, N.Y.: Orbis Books, 1989), 103.

10. Ibid.

11. In English "mystique," from the French *mystique,* is used as the equivalent of *mística.* See Renny Golden, *The Hour of the Poor, the Hour of Women* (New York: Crossroad, 1991), 17. In the unpublished proposal for her dissertation Sister Gay Redmond used Durkheim's insights on "effervescence" to explain *mística.* See Emile Durkheim, *The Elementary Forms of Religious Life,* trans. Joseph Ward (New York: Free Press, 1965), 257–61.

After-Words

I always tell the students I work with that the main quality of a good ethicist, of a good moral theologian, is humility — that we need to accept the fact that our understanding is always limited, and that, therefore, we need to say to ourselves time and time again, "This is the best I can do right now; this is the best way I can say it and do it right now." Then we have to pray that next time around we will do it better, say it better. This is the spirit with which I come to the end of this book.

My attempt in pulling together these essays has been to give a voice, a public voice, to Latina women, including myself. My goal has been to contribute to our struggle for liberation, to *la lucha*. I cannot conceptualize liberation apart from salvation; I cannot think of justice apart from grace; I cannot think of being kin to God, of being part of God's kin without being in solidarity with the poor and the oppressed. Therefore I do hope that this book makes a small but valuable contribution to *la lucha*, to the struggle for justice, to the unfolding of the kin-dom of God.

I understand *mujerista* theology as a process, a process of conscientization, a process of self-identification and self-definition for Latinas. Therefore, in no way is this book "conclusive." After each of the essays included here I could write many questions that arise from what I say, that need to be explored further, that we need to talk about with other Latinas, that need to be answered in the future. There are three specific areas that need further elaboration that clearly arise from what I say in this book. The first one is embodiment. The issue of who we are as Latinas cannot be dealt with apart from our bodies. How do we relate to our bodies? How are we oppressed precisely through and because of our bodies? What are the cultural-religious resources Latinas use to live "with" their bodies, given that our bodies are used against us? The issues around embodiment are immensely important. I am part of a team of six Latinas hard at work now on this issue. Yes, even as I write this, we are in the process of gathering with groups of Latinas around the country to reflect on "embodiment."

The second theme that needs further exploration is "family." Family is at the heart of Latino culture, and because Latinas play a central role in it and are held more responsible than men are for it, *mujerista* theology has to elaborate a liberative discourse about family from the perspective of grassroots Latinas. The politics of family — how family is understood and how it is "used" by churches, politics, and social institutions — are extremely complicated. I must confess that it scares me to deal with "family," but then, being courageous is a matter of going ahead in spite of being afraid.

The third theme is justice. Justice is an intrinsic element of the gospel message; justice is at the heart of all liberative praxis. Therefore, in *mujerista* theology we always need to work more with this theme. The incarnation of justice is what our liberative vision is all about. Justice is what grounds and is the goal of our *proyecto histórico*, our historical project. Justice is what makes us insist that the goal of *mujerista* theology is radical structural change and not mere participation in oppressive structures. The commitment to justice is what clarifies our strategies and forces us to make options that will contribute to the unfolding of the kin-dom of God. So we always have to clarify further what we mean by justice. In *mujerista* theology there is always the need to better understand and explain justice, for it is the commitment to justice that makes it possible to believe and proclaim with joy that to struggle is to live, *la vida es la lucha*.

Index

African religions, 74, 194
  mestiza and *mulata* Christianity
    and, 149, 159, 189
Amerindian religions, 74, 194
  mestiza and *mulata* Christianity
    and, 149, 159, 189
Anselm, Saint, 124
Anthropology, *mujerista*, 128
ASPIRA, 135

Babylonian exiles, 42–43
Bible, 148–58, 177
  as an interpretive key, 161–65
  liberative praxis and, 158–61
Brueggemann, Walter, 44, 45,
  46–47

Chávez, César, 135
Christ. *See* Jesus
Christianity
  Hispanic culture and, 62
  of Latinas, 74
  mestiza and *mulata*, 149, 159,
    189
  sixteenth-century Spanish,
    74
Classism, 40–41
Comadrazgo, 140–41
Compadrazgo, 140–41
Conquistadores, 149, 189
Conscientization
  Bible and, 161
  mutuality and, 94–95
Cotidiano, lo, 66–73, 131, 134
Cubans, 46–49, 64
Cultural imperialism, 113–14

Deuteronomy 32:35, 45
Differences
  justice and, 118–19
  in theology, 79–82

Ecumenism, 155
Edomites, 44
Education, 157–58
"El Son de las Tres Décadas,"
  48–53
Epistemological vigilance, 76–77
Ethnic prejudice, 41
  cultural imperialism and,
    113–14
  in feminist movement, 18–21
Eucharist, 171, 176
Exiles, 47–48
Exodus 1:15–22, 162–65
Exploitation, 110–11

Faith, 30
Familia/comunidad, 128, 137–44
Feminists, Euro-American,
    racism/ethnic prejudice
    of, 18–21
Fiestas, 130–31
Freire, Paulo, 95
God, 164
  cotidiano, lo, and, 71
  fear of, 163
  Jesus' suffering and, 130
  language of vengeance and, 45
  Latinas' relationship with,
    62–63, 174–76, 198
  salvation and, 89
  sin and, 90
  traditional theology and, 78, 79